THE LIVES AND LEGACIES
OF EVERYDAY HEROES

Unlimited Publishing LLC ("UP") provides worldwide book design, printing, marketing and distribution services for authors and publishers. UP does not exercise editorial control over books. Sole responsibility for the content of each work rests with the author(s) and/or contributing publisher(s) and not with UP. The opinions expressed herein may not be interpreted in any way as representing those of UP, nor any of its affiliates.

THE LIVES AND LEGACIES OF EVERYDAY HEROES

BY

DR. MARK J. BRITZMAN, ED.D.

Unlimited Publishing
Bloomington, Indiana

ACKNOWLEDGEMENTS

To my wife and best friend, Rhonda, who is my everyday hero because of her steady stream of love, laughter, caring, energy, responsibility, and community involvement,

To my daughters, Kylee and Ali, who remind me each day of the amazing beauty of God's creations,

To my parents, Dar and Jo, who continue to give me all the love, stability, and encouragement I would ever need to be a good person and make a positive difference in the lives of others,

To Neil Salkind, Ph.D., my literary agent, and Susan Gilbert-Collins, my copy editor, who helped make this book a reality,

To Michael Josephson, founder and president of the Josephson Institute of Ethics and CHARACTER COUNTS! program, who has provided me with the challenge, understanding, and inspiration to become a better person and encourage others to do the same,

To the authors of the "everyday hero" stories in this book who took the time and effort to inspire others to greater heights of character, …

The world is a better place because of your existence and resulting contributions!

CONTENTS

FOREWORD
By Michael Josephson

Heraclitus declared that our character determines our destiny. Martin Luther King spoke of the importance of judging others by the content of their character. And more and more, we hear about the "character issue" in modern elections. Yet, scanning any day's news leads us to believe that character is a rare commodity. As Lily Tomlin said, "No matter how cynical I get, I can't keep up."

In collecting these original stories by ordinary people about the people who influenced their lives with the strength of character, Mark Britzman offers us a powerful rebuttal to cynicism about human nature. He provides tangible evidence that the world is full of people of character, everyday heroes that uplift and strengthen those they touch.

This book presents us with a mosaic of life-changing relationships. While each story has its own charm or insight, together they present a vision of humanity that is both inspiring and profound. There is both responsibility and opportunity in the realization that every one of us has the capacity to affect all eternity through the lessons we teach through our words and actions.

The once powerful observation that one person can make a difference has become so much of a cliché that we sometimes lose sight of the intrinsic truth and importance of this indisputable fact. Each tale in *Everyday Heroes* reveals another example of one person permanently shaping the values and attitudes of another simply by the force of their character.

It's likely that most of the everyday heroes who helped sculpt the stone that would become the character of their child, spouse, friend or student had no idea of the significance of their impact. Unless we are told, how can any of us know the effect we have on others?

This book teaches us that what we say and do and, most importantly, who we are, does make a difference and that compassion and courage, tenderness and tenacity, honesty and integrity are the stuff of true heroes.

We have become a country that seems to delight in identifying and then eating those we called our heroes. We moan about the absence of great leaders, claiming to want heroes for ourselves and role models for our children. Yet we are quick to throw them to the lions when we see a flaw or weakness. Instead of being uplifted and inspired by integrity, honor, compassion or courage, we seem to feel threatened by the very idea that it's possible to live more nobly than we do.

Mark Britzman teaches us that you don't have to be perfect to be a hero to someone and that heroes are not necessarily extraordinary people. They are simply people who make an extraordinary impact on someone else. He encourages us to recognize the heroes of our lives. They are probably not celebrities and it's not likely that they earned their status through some extraordinary act of bravery or nobility. More likely they are parents or spouses, friends or teachers, people who came into our lives without a drum roll and whose stripes were earned in the trenches of everyday living.

1. The Lives Of "Everyday Heroes"

"The real test of character is whether we are willing to the right thing when it costs more than we want to pay."
— Michael Josephson

My daughter was uncharacteristically quiet in the car after I picked her up from school. I had expected her to be excited about finishing the last day of first grade and embarking on a summer of fun. As I looked over to try to make sense of her unusual silence, I noticed tears streaming down her cheeks.

"Kylee, what's wrong?"

She was choked up but managed to say, "Daddy, I can't stop thinking about it."

"What happened, sweetie?" I asked anxiously, wondering what possible trauma she had endured.

Kylee said, "I just can't stop thinking that I will never have my first grade teacher ever again." My concern quickly dissolved into relief and understanding. The pain on her face was the result of missing someone who had become very important in her life.

At that moment, I realized what a tremendous impact an adult can have on a child. I have now come to expect this response at the end of every school year because every teacher has become an everyday hero to Kylee. Her sister, Ali, had a similar response as she just completed her first year of school. My children's growth and development have also been shaped by many other caring adults including, but not limited to, their grandparents, relatives, pastor, Sunday school teachers, camp counselors, neighbors, and most importantly, their mother and me.

Most middle school and high school students probably do not go through an intense grieving response at the end of the school year; they probably do not shed too many tears when the last day of school rolls around. However, they, too, need healthy role models in their lives. Every adult has the potential to significantly influence a youngster in a positive manner, becoming a teacher of good character. As Henry Adams stated, "Teachers affect all eternity...you never know where their influence stops."

Unfortunately, too many youngsters do not have positive role models in their lives. When I recently asked the fourth-grade girls basketball team that I coach who they admired most in their lives, one girl looked at me and said, "I don't trust anyone!" Too many of our youth do not have positive role models and as a result become morally confused and susceptible to unhealthy influences. The result of growing up in moral poverty is typically a selfish philosophy that justifies nearly any self-serving behavior, regardless of how it affects others.

This growing hole in the moral ozone has been confirmed by research. According to a recent survey of 20,879 randomly sampled middle school and high school students conducted by the Josephson Institute of Ethics, 47% of the students admitted they had stolen something from a store within the past year. Seventy percent confessed to cheating at least once in the past year. And despite this, 91% stated that they were satisfied with their own ethics and character.

In response to mounting evidence of this moral decay, an eminent and diverse group of educators, youth leaders, and ethicists spent three and a half days in Aspen, Colorado, and looked for solutions. The group knew that good people could disagree regarding complex ethical questions; however, there had to be some common framework that could be agreed upon.

They issued the Aspen Declaration, which states the following:

1) The next generation will be the stewards of our communities, nation, and planet in extraordinarily critical times.

2) The present and future well-being of our society requires an involved, caring citizenry with good moral character.

3) People do not automatically develop good moral character; therefore, conscientious efforts must be made to instruct young people in the values and abilities necessary for moral decision making and conduct.

4) Effective character education is based on core ethical values rooted in democratic society, in particular, respect, responsibility, trustworthiness, caring, fairness, and good citizenship.

5) These core ethical values transcend cultural, religious, and socioeconomic differences.

6) Character education is, first and foremost, an obligation of families and faith communities, but schools and youth-serving organizations also have responsibility to help develop the character of young people.

7) These responsibilities are best achieved when these groups work in concert.

8) Finally, the character and conduct of our youth reflect the character and conduct of society; therefore, every adult has the responsibility to teach and model the core ethical values, and every social institution has the responsibility to promote the development of good character.

The core ethical values they agreed upon have become the six pillars of character. They include trustworthiness, respect, responsibility, fairness, caring, and good citizenship. These words were good enough to become agreed-upon values to teach, advocate, model, and enforce at home, school, church, youth organizations, and at work.

A grassroots initiative referred to as CHARACTER COUNTS! was born following the Aspen Conference and has quickly become the nation's most widely used character-development framework, adopted by schools as well as numerous organizations around the United States and beyond. One encouraging statistic is that 97% of youngsters polled acknowledged that it is important for them to be persons of good character! The hope for the future is that wherever they are — at home, school, church, or athletics — our youth will have everyday heroes that will model the six pillars of character and challenge them to live accordingly.

It is easy to blame our youth for not living up to our expectations. But while they do need to take responsibility for their behavior, it is clear that they have simply been expressing themselves in reaction to the moral vacuum we adults have created for them. Our society has become so reluctant to endorse any values in particular that children too often grow up in moral poverty. As a result, they acquire a mind-set of entitlement. That is, "What's in it for me?" Michael Josephson, the founder of the CHARACTER COUNTS! coalition, describes this as the "I Deserve It Creed" that claims, "Whatever I want, I need. Whatever I need, I deserve. Whatever I deserve, I have a right to have — and I'll do anything to get it." Josephson elaborates that when challenged, individuals often respond with the mentality commonly referred to as the "doctrine of relative filth": "I'm not so bad as long as other people are worse."

Rationalizations such as this become roadblocks to ethical behavior. Furthermore, we have become so obsessed with making certain that our children are happy and have high self-esteem that we fail to first establish a moral foundation. It should come as no surprise that our young people are making more unhealthy choices now than at any other time in our history. Instead of putting the self above all else, our efforts should be focused on sending the following message: "First, do no harm; secondly, be good; and lastly, be happy."

No one is immune from the consequences if our young people's characters continue to erode; just one person willing to act irresponsibly can change the lives of many others. My wife recently received the type of phone call that turns every parent's worst fear into a reality. "Rhonda, there was an accident and Kylee was involved. You'd better come as quickly as you can." My wife hung up the phone and told me to drive to the scene while she took care of our other daughter to protect her from the trauma of possibly witnessing a terrible accident. As I approached the accident, my heart began to race. The police had blocked off the busy street, and there appeared to be numerous fire trucks and ambulances. I quickly parked the car and ran toward the brutal four-car pile-up. Suddenly a woman called to me and said, "Mark, I've been looking for you and want you to know that your daughter is physically okay. We've been keeping her warm in our van, and my son is currently talking to her." I remember thinking, *Thank God!* However, there were others less fortunate. Although there were no fatalities, individuals were being rushed off to the hospital bleeding and unconscious.

What caused the accident? A high school senior had been speeding that Monday evening and smacked the car he was driving into the car driven by our friend who was taking her two children and Kylee to dance class. The impact jolted their car into oncoming traffic in the other lane and resulted in a four-car accident. One bad choice by an indifferent high school senior negatively impacted numerous people.

My wife and I, like most parents, take parenting and family life very seriously. Although we make mistakes, Rhonda and I would do anything to help Kylee and Ali thrive. However, it is not enough just to have a healthy family. All of our children will sooner or later peddle their bikes into the larger community — and hopefully, that community will be a healthy one. As psychologist and author Mary Pipher stated, "a healthy family member entering an unhealthy community environment is like someone standing on the first class deck of the Titanic as it sinks to the bottom. Our world needs healthy individuals, families, *and* communities."

Doing the right thing is relatively easy if it seems to serve one's purposes to do so. But what if being ethical comes with a price? Would that high school student who caused the accident be willing to follow the speed limit even if it meant he would be late to a very important date? Many of us can probably be persuaded to follow the speed limit if we're not in a hurry — or if we see a policeman! But what if we're late to a job interview, and the law isn't looking? These situations are the true test of our character. Are we willing to do the right thing even if it costs us more than we want to pay? Thomas Lickona, the well-respected developmental psychologist and character educator, defines character as "knowing the good, loving the good, and doing the good." It entails ethical behavior in action. Persons of great character are, of course, not perfect. However, they own up to and learn from past mistakes and work hard to do better the next day.

Most of us, after all, are ethical in our own eyes. How often have you heard a person say, *I'm basically a good person*? The word "basically" becomes extremely important. *I'm a good person unless it becomes disadvantageous for me to be a good person.* What is your threshold? Have you ever been in a grocery store and snuck into the ten-item or less checkout lane with more than ten items? Have you ever completed a tax return with unrevealed income? What about talking behind someone's back? Or stopping at a four-way stop and proceeding before it was your turn? Have you ever worked less productively when your supervisor was away on vacation? Or taken the last cup of coffee at work and left, hoping someone else would brew a new pot? You get the idea. I believe that you, like I, know what the right thing to do is in all of the above situations. The real test of our character is not our good intentions or justifications but rather our final decisions.

The key to making good decisions is living by the six pillars. Think about the many individuals in your life and how they measure up to these pillars. Whom do you trust the most? Everyday heroes earn your trust by not talking behind your back, following through on commitments, telling the truth, having a high level of integrity, and being loyal in good times and bad. This trust is crucial in developing enduring and rewarding personal relationships in all areas of life. Deceptions, lies, and unreliable behavior lead to cracks in the foundation of meaningful personal and professional relationships. Individuals who are trustworthy are true to themselves and live up to their highest and best personal values. Trustworthy individuals do not tolerate exaggerations, false promises, deliberate distortions, or concealment of facts. These are all considered lies. Keeping your word, honoring commitments, being prepared, and being loyal to the person not present are all essential ingredients that enhance trust.

Everyday heroes are also respectful. The essence of respect is to treat others as social equals and have positive regard for the dignity of all people, including oneself. Respectful behavior includes living by the golden rule, respecting privacy and freedom, being courteous and polite, and tolerating and accepting differences. Intolerance, prejudice, and discrimination are obviously disrespectful. More specifically, respectful behavior can entail seeking first to understand others, encouraging input from others, and resolving differences in an assertive yet compassionate manner.

Everyday heroes are responsible for their attitudes and choices. Being responsible entails being in charge of our choices and thus, our lives. We are morally responsible for the consequences of all of our choices. This means doing our duty, being accountable, pursuing excellence, and exercising self-control. Everything we do makes a difference and starts a chain reaction that affects the lives of others. Responsible people refrain from blaming others or making excuses for their actions and in-actions. They see the world as offering infinite possibilities and incorporate a "can-do" attitude.

Everyday heroes make every effort to be fair. Individuals that are fair ensure the likelihood that the process and result of every decision is just to those affected. Fairness includes giving proper notice, being impartial, gathering the facts, and ensuring an appropriate decision-making process. A just person is never knowingly unfair.

Everyday heroes model the pillar of caring. Caring individuals do their best to bring out the best in others. They are compassionate, empathetic, kind, loving, considerate, thankful, and forgiving. Uncaring behaviors include being mean, being cruel, being insensitive, being self-centered, or being too busy getting ahead at the expense of others. Caring means more, however, than a concern for the well-being of oneself and others. Caring also includes a passion about making the world a better place to live.

Everyday heroes make a contribution to society by being good citizens. They work hard to fulfill their civic duties, respect authority and law, and attempt to make the world a better place, understanding that the human condition is inter-connected. They realize that the most important political office is that of private citizen. As a result, they give of themselves and their resources in a joyous yet sacrificial manner.

These fundamental truths, when put into action, act as the springboard for making choices that benefit society. They are easy words to talk about but much more challenging to live by. The good news is, however, that you do not have to be great-looking, rich, or have high self-esteem to be an everyday hero.

When making ethical decisions, the everyday hero thinks about how his or her decision will impact others. Everyday heroes anticipate whether a decision will enhance trust, respect, responsibility, caring, fairness, and citizenship. And when these pillars are in conflict with each other, they make the decision that will benefit society in the long run. That is, if everybody made the same decision, would it be a good thing?

Unfortunately, everyday heroes are too often overlooked in our society. This book introduces and applauds just a few individuals who possess great character and have important legacies to pass on. These everyday heroes bring a sense of decency into our lives. They are the individuals we all want as family members, friends, neighbors, teachers, colleagues, or mentors. And they can inspire us to be everyday heroes ourselves.

II. The Everyday Heroes of Working Professionals

MY EVERYDAY HERO
By David Tingle

One of Webster's definitions for "pilot" is: *"To act as a guide; to lead or conduct over a usually difficult course."*

I found this definition to be particularly appropriate regarding my "Everyday Hero" because not only did my everyday hero act as a guide to help lead me over a usually difficult course (growing up), but he was also a pilot by profession.

I was the youngest of three children. My two sisters were seven and eight years older than I. Both sisters had graduated from high school and gone on to college before I reached seventh grade.

The summer after I completed eighth grade, my oldest sister met a man that she felt was special. He was several years older than she was, divorced, and had custody of his two children. He was a pilot for a company that built large custom grain storage facilities. She called and invited my parents and me to come down for the weekend to meet him. She had a history of boyfriends that didn't meet with my father's approval, and Dad was skeptical about this one as well.

As it turned out, a couple who had been long-time friends of my parents were also going to be in that town that weekend, so visiting plans fell into place, and we went down for the weekend. I don't remember much about the pilot from that first night, as it was around supper time when we got to the town where my sisters were going to college, and he joined us later. It turned into a late night. I vaguely remember Dad, his friend, and the pilot discussing the merits of an early round of golf the next morning. I remember Dad joking to his friend back at the motel later that night that he'd be mighty surprised if we saw anything of the pilot and his golf clubs any time before noon.

At 7:00 that next morning, there was a gentle knock at the door. Mom opened it, and there he stood, golf clubs in hand, ready to go. Dad scrambled for the phone to call his buddy in the next room, and about 15 minutes later, they left to go golfing.

After they returned, I could tell that dad thought that the pilot was a pretty decent sort. His name was Dick Bierman, he had two children named Rick and Kendra, and he lived in Kearney. I'm not sure if I saw any more of him that weekend or not, but I am sure that neither of us knew at that time what a huge role he would end up playing in my life.

That October, I had my 15th birthday. Dick flew both my sisters up for the day. As a special surprise, Dick took a friend and me up for an airplane ride over our town. I had never been in a small plane before, and it was a fantastic experience. Dick did some mild aerobatics with the plane, and when I encouraged him to do some more, he said, "There are old pilots, and there are bold pilots, but there's no such thing as an old, bold pilot." I agreed.

I saw Dick a few more times that fall as he came up for opening day of pheasant season and later for Thanksgiving. Christmas came and went, and then came the new year, 1977. Wednesday evening, January 5th, my mom, youngest sister, and me had been uptown shopping and running errands. Oddly, my mom's sister and her husband ran into us and told us to stop by my mom's parents' house on the way home. This seemed a little odd, but we obliged and went to the house with them. My uncle said something to my mom about "getting ready for a shock" as she opened the door. When we stepped in, I could tell something wasn't right. Grandpa and Grandma were sitting in their chairs, shaking and dabbing at their eyes with tissues, and there was a man there that I knew to be the hospital chaplain. My first thought was that Grandpa, who had emphysema, was dying. Then I looked up, and a friend of my dad's was standing there, quietly looking at me. As my eyes met his, I saw a single tear run down his cheek, and like a bolt of lightning, it struck me that Dad was not there. I was then informed that he had died from an unexpected, massive heart attack. I have never felt so alone or scared as I did at that moment.

The rest of that evening was a blur, but somehow, I managed to fall asleep on my grandparents' couch. The next morning I awoke and for a few moments didn't remember the agony of the night before. Then it all came back. I opened my eyes, and there was Dick sitting on a chair next to me.

"How are you doing, pal?" he asked, and I fell apart all over again. He talked to me for a while, and I felt better. I began to realize that things would be all right, and that, somehow, I would make it through this ordeal.

At Dad's funeral, I struggled to maintain my composure throughout the service. As the service concluded and my family started down the aisle to leave, the finality of the events at hand overwhelmed me, and I started to fall apart again. A caring arm and shoulder in a brown jacket steadied me as I stumbled toward the exit. It was Dick. From that moment on, whenever I felt I was "stumbling" in my life, he was there. And things always ended up being okay.

Over the course of the next several months, he and my sister announced their plans to marry, and I was ecstatic. I had gotten to know Dick well and had grown very fond of him. He was very good to my sister, and they were happy together.

One of the first things I noticed about Dick was that he had a lot of ambition. If something needed to be done, he was on it and had it finished in short order. He helped out around the house a lot and always had a neat, tidy yard. He was very efficient and liked keeping things well organized.

He was not afraid to tackle sizable projects either. I remember the time my grandparents' trees in their yard needed to be trimmed. The trees were large red and silver maples that had become overgrown. They were well beyond my capabilities and my grandpa's capabilities, too.

But not Dick's. The next time he and my sister came down to visit, he was prepared. I'll never forget the way he climbed up those trees with the chain saw and the pruning shears and started trimming away. In about an hour, he had trimmed and shaped all four of the red maples and had cut back the branches on the three silver maples that were hanging over the house. Then he cut up and stacked the logs and branches by the curb to be hauled away.

Over the next few years, he and my sister had two more children, Rhett and Kourtney. It was not uncommon to see Dick changing diapers and giving baths to the two little ones and helping the two older kids with their homework. Although he was very good-natured, he knew how to be firm when it came to discipline, and I respected him for that. I could tell his kids did, too. I don't recall him ever spanking his children, but he never really needed to. He had a way of communicating on their own level about right and wrong. Despite that firmness, he always showed them how much he loved them. And they loved him, too.

Dick had his life under control. I don't remember ever seeing him even come close to losing his composure, despite going through some challenging times. When he got laid off from the flight department at the insurance company, he calmly made some phone calls, had a few interviews and test flights, and within a matter of a couple of weeks, he was flying for Long Lines, LTD, a progressive telecommunications firm.

A few years later, Dick faced another challenge. A nagging cough had turned into pneumonia. During examination of his x-rays, the doctors noticed something unusual on his left lung. A biopsy was ordered, and it came back positive. Although Dick had not smoked for over nine years, he now had lung cancer. Surgery was scheduled immediately, and the doctors removed half of his left lung.

I went over to see him just after he got home from the hospital. He pulled up his tee-shirt and showed me the scar. It started on his chest just below the sternum and followed the bottom left edge of his ribcage around his side, and finally ran partway up his back, ending about six inches from his spine. I couldn't believe it. He talked about the procedure as I would have talked about having my teeth cleaned. He was already looking forward to flying again. True to form, he healed up quickly and in short order was back in the air. I guess none of us realized the seriousness of this illness because it didn't really seem to slow him down, and he flew for another three years.

Then it came back. Fast and furious the cancer swept along, determined to finish what it had started. Over a couple of months, Dick lost over 30 pounds and was unable to continue flying. Because he had beaten this beast before, we prayed for a miracle again. He and my sister went to the Mayo Clinic for evaluation, and their oldest son joined my wife and me in visiting them for the weekend. Although he was in a lot of pain, he was his usual upbeat, jovial self, and like always, he had a few funny stories for me. He never uttered so much as a whimper about the pain he was in. We all enjoyed a nice dinner that night, and we went back home the next day, leaving my sister and him there.

That next night, Dick's condition deteriorated rapidly, and he slipped into a coma. My sister called the next morning to tell us what happened. As we got ready to head back to Rochester, the realization that we were going to lose Dick began to sink in. That same scared, lost feeling I had when my dad died came back.

We arrived in Rochester, and Dick was starting to come out of the coma. I cannot describe the agony and hopelessness we felt as we gathered outside his room. The doctors kept him sedated as they examined him.

The next morning, he was not strongly sedated and wanted to see all of us. Since he was on the ventilator, he couldn't talk, but he could write. And write he did. He told a few funny stories, we laughed about some of our hunting escapades, and for a while, I think we all forgot about what kind of situation he was in. But that was just Dick's style. He didn't complain or dwell on his situation. In fact, he didn't even make reference to it until the end of the day when his writings turned insightful. In his own special way, he began telling each of us good-bye.

He thanked us for being his family and for being there with him. He wished his kids good luck and asked them to be good for their mother. He asked me to help keep an eye on his kids. One of the last things he wrote that evening was that we should not be sad for him because he was going to go on to heaven, and he would see us all again.

Later that night, Dick slipped into a coma from which he never awoke. He died three days later.

I could fill volumes about what I learned from my hero, the pilot. He lived his life to the fullest, and his priorities were his family and his faith. He had an unshakable faith from which he drew his strengths, and this was never more evident than in his final hours on earth. Dick had a way of picking up people's spirits just by being around. From his travels as a pilot, he always managed to collect a few jokes and funny stories to tell. Life to him was an adventure, and he believed in enjoying the journey. He knew how to work when work needed to be done, and he knew how to play when it was time to play.

Since Dick's passing, I have become a father three times. I am trying to be as good a father to my kids and as good a husband to my wife as Dick was for his kids and his wife. I am trying to face my adversities with the same kind of strength with which Dick faced his.

And I am looking forward to that day when he and I will meet again.

MY EVERYDAY HERO
By Rita Weber

My mother was a strong woman, both physically and emotionally. A neighbor down the road claimed that she had once single-handedly lifted up the rear end of a car when there was no jack available. She was quick to deny that any such thing had happened, but seeing her rise to whatever challenge came her way made one wonder if it might not be true.

With this belief in her unshakable capacity to handle life, it was unnerving to witness the events that transpired one winter day long ago. Our strong and steadfast mother bared her soul before us, revealing a vulnerable, fragile self within.

It was very early on a February morning and the house was still bitterly cold. Two of my sisters and I were snuggled up together in the big double bed when our older brother, Danny, came in, whispering urgently.

"Wake up! Wake up!" He shook us. "You need to get up!"

"Leave me alone. I'm tired," I moaned, trying to roll over and bury my head in the pillow.

"No!" he insisted, still in that insistent whisper. "Dad's been in an accident and you need to get up!"

"Oh, yeah, I'm sure," I began to scoff, when my attention shifted from Danny to something I had never heard before. It was my mother weeping, sobbing from the very depths of her soul. The sound was coming from the kitchen, just outside our room, and I sat up in bed for a while, listening intently to see if I could make any sense of what was going on.

"Oh, God, no!" I heard her wail. "Why now? Why did this have to happen?"

I slid down off the bed, unaware of the coldness of the floor. As I walked into the light of the kitchen, I saw her sitting there with her head in her hands. She was weeping and moaning, oblivious to anyone or anything around her.

I tried to approach her, but I had no idea what to do. I had never seen her cry before. I had never seen anyone, in all my eight years, cry like that before.

My older brothers appeared on the scene, slipping into the roles of adulthood, even though they were only teenagers themselves. They explained about Dad's accident, there in the thick fog of that fateful day. He had been riding to his work as a bricklayer in his friend Roy's car. They had been only a couple of miles from home when they crashed into a train stalled on the tracks. There were no flares or warning. By the time they could see it, it was too late. Dad had been thrown out of the windshield and was lying now, unconscious, in the hospital. While mom stayed at the hospital, our neighbor next door would came to stay with us.

Seven weeks went by and Dad was released from the hospital. He was different, though. He hobbled uncertainly on the crutches that would remain part of life for him. Whether from the head injury, the medications he was given, or the serious depression that engulfed him, his return home was not a joyful time. He could stand none of the noise that comes with six children in the house. He felt worthless and spent much of his time in bed or in the city seeing specialists, hoping to recover some of what he had lost. For a year following the accident, his condition demanded extensive dental work, massive numbers of pills, and my mother's attention and care.

It was a year of scant income. There was no such thing as Medicaid to help us through. My brothers' earnings from helping out on nearby farms was the only income our family had. We survived on a diet of mostly potatoes. It was a hard year.

After a settlement was reached with the insurance company, my parents bought a small country store. Mom wanted to be home with us, but she needed to be able to support us, too. It seemed like the best option available to them.

We were excited to hear that we would soon be moving. The store had living quarters above it where we would live. Some of our hope had been restored.

We drove to our new home, located amongst a small cluster of buildings known as West Albion. A community hall, a creamery, and five or so houses neatly lined the widened area of the road. A two-story framed building, identified proudly by a hand-painted sign over the door as "West Albion Country Store," stood right in the middle of it all.

This little hub of activity was similar to many other country stores that dotted the landscape a few decades ago. The store carried a little bit of everything, from milk to tennis shoes, shotgun shells to toiletries. Its wooden floors smelled of pine cleaner and the door had a bell that would ring when a customer walked through it. The store enjoyed a steady stream of traffic—men running in to pay for the gas they had just pumped or someone stopping by for bread or milk or meat.

"Would you put that on my bill, Hazel?" folks could often be heard to say. Mother would nod, and the person would smile and wave and head on their way.

This way of doing business was pretty unremarkable for that time and place. Credit in the farmland had been a part of things for a long time, and even though Mom did not know each person by name when she first opened the store, it was not long until she knew them not only by name but as individuals, unique and special. No, the store was not remarkable, but Mom was.

At first glance, her appearance did not reveal this. Mom was a good-sized woman, always wearing one of her familiar cotton housedresses with an apron over it, handmade by my grandma. Her hair, carefully washed and curled for Sundays, held its permanent curls throughout the week, combed, but not coifed.

She was always busy, even when sitting down behind the counter between customers. There were order forms to fill out and books to reconcile. But as soon as the door opened, she stopped what she was doing, smiled, and greeted the person coming in. When necessary, she would switch over to Finnish, in which she was as fluent as English.

People would come to the store to sip on a bottle of pop, relax on the long oak bench, and bare their souls to this caring woman behind the counter. Old men, children, young housewives — all came, drawn by her gentle manner, her kind and patient listening, and her carefully shared truths.

There was never a question about where she stood on things. A quick glance around the store gave a person instant insight into her philosophy of life. "Praise the Lord ANYWAY!" was mounted on the scale where the pork chops had to be weighed. "Count it ALL joy!" was there on the front of the cash register. The signs were not very large in size, but they were huge in impact, opening doors for Mom to share about the faith that had sustained her through the good times and the bad. Furthermore, she had the kind of personal witness that needed no defense; an observation of the way she lived soon revealed that her faith was real.

Dad's disability at age 44 had left her to be the sole breadwinner for the six of seven children who were still at home. In addition to working in the store from 6 a.m. to 9 p.m., she had to do all the household duties and child care.

The store was never open on Sundays; that was the Lord's day of rest. It also closed at 6:30 every Thursday night so all of us could go to the midweek Bible study. On Saturday nights after the store had closed, Mom would wash her hair, prepare the Sunday School lesson, and watch the late movie on television with her family. Then she would be up early on Sunday to make breakfast, get everyone ready for church, and prepare a wonderful Sunday dinner, usually for her family and a few guests. It was only after finishing dinner and visiting for a while that she would take a Sunday nap — rising again to go for a ride with her family and make supper before returning to church Sunday evening.

Growing up, I took for granted the tremendous energy that she had. She never said she was tired or complained that she didn't feel like working. She just did things, one after another, always with great speed but never rushed.

She was never preachy, but she repeated Bible verses often, maybe as much for herself as for us kids. "I can do all things through Christ," or "All things work together for good to them that love God." These were her promises, the affirmations that she chose to live by.

She was a mother who had to be shared — with people of the community who came to the store, with visitors to our home, with members of our church. Yet she always made me feel that she had time to listen to anything I needed to say. When I spoke about things at school or talked about what I thought of an idea or happening in the world, she listened carefully to what I said, shared her thoughts in a respectful way, and never demanded that I change my viewpoint. She accepted that I had opinions and that I had a right to them.

This dear woman molded and shaped the world around her with the positive example of her life. She continues to live on in the lives of her seven children and numerous grandchildren. And just as importantly, she lives on in the lives of all those whose hearts she touched from behind the counter.

MY EVERYDAY HERO
By Mike Simpkins

There are few things more intimidating to a growing boy than Little League baseball. Your legs are growing at one rate while your arms have chosen another — all the while leaving your head and heart in the dust as they try to catch up. I was one of those growing-in-all-directions kids at age eleven, and I was fortunate to be in good company, as everyone on my team was pretty evenly matched. None of us felt too inadequate. I'd played a couple of seasons with the same guys, and we all knew that we were near the bottom of our Little League hierarchy. Then I met Clay.

Clay, short for "Clayton," was a kid from Arkansas and spoke a foreign accent to those of us in Montana. I'd never met anyone named Clayton before. Neither had the team, and we weren't very forgiving. He was the odd man out, an implant to our neighborhood, without the rights that would go to a cousin or even just a friend of one of the guys on the team. He was short, a bit tubby, and took forever to get out simple phrases — as if his southern drawl had made him the tortoise and we the northern hares. Our rapid boy-speak exchanges were punctuated by the slow, steady additions from our southern teammate. But once we put him on the ball field, we all got a case of, "Well, shut my mouth!" He was our star — throwing farther and catching better than any of us could. It was our first practice of the season, and we all knew that with Clay's help, we might even win a game.

And then he took off his ball glove to get ready to bat. The questions started flying. "Hey, what happened to your hand? You only got three fingers!" It was true. Through some stroke of fate, Clay had been born with a thumb — if you could call it that -and two other fingers on his glove hand. They were knobby, stumpy things, as if someone had duct-taped his first and second fingers together and then done the same with his third and fourth (little) finger. He looked like an alien, or better yet, a three-toed sloth (I was proud of that observation and shared it in laughter with the team). Our probing and teasing didn't seem to matter to him a bit; he just took it all in. He even laughed. "Hadn't ever heard about the sloth thing before," he chuckled and picked up his bat. He answered our questions with a grin before he walked out to the plate.

After his third line drive to center field (sailing just over the shortstop's head and landing just out of the center fielder's area of coverage), we forgot about the sloth thing. We marveled in his ability to place his hits anywhere on the field he wanted. He was awesome, and I knew I had treated him poorly.

After practice, Clay came up to me and asked me where I lived. We rode bikes to my house and played catch in my backyard. We became friends quickly. Each day after practice or a game, we'd find time to hone our baseball skills at my house or down the street at the park. He taught me more about baseball than my father had and all with that gentle, good humor God had given him. He told me to throw the way it worked for me: "Well, God made a ton of people—but just one of you." I never became a baseball great, but I learned how to throw, catch, and hit as well as any of my teammates. We lost a lot of ball games over the season, but it didn't seem to bother Clay at all. "Well, we could quit," he'd say, "but that'd be silly." We all kept playing and even won a few games every now and then.

Baseball was our passion, but we found time for other things. I remember fishing with Clay at Holter Lake between Helena and Great Falls nestled in the mountains near Wolf Creek. My father and older brother liked to fish below the dam, and Clay and I were bored. We'd already climbed all of the huge boulders strewn about below the dam, and we were hunting for new thrills to be had. "Let's climb that cliff!" I said, pointing to the wall of shale and grass rising sixty feet above us. So we did. Clay made it right up to the top while I slipped near the top and found myself hanging on for dear life to a matted clump of weeds and grasses. "You can do it," he drawled, "jes' git on climbing." He was calm and so sure of my ability that I believed him. I made it and wondered at the top how it was I hadn't fallen to the boulders below. Clay just said, "That was good climbing. I knew you'd make it."

That summer, we played ball together, went fishing and camping, climbed more cliffs, and got into trouble as kids will do. And then he went back to Arkansas. Clay was the son of divorced parents and had only been visiting his dad for the summer. I promised to stay in touch, but I didn't. His dad was a military man and got transferred that fall, so he didn't come back to Montana. I haven't spoken to him since we said good-bye over twenty-five years ago.

I think about him often, though. Every time I go rock climbing today, I think of him standing up at the top saying, "You can do it, jes' git on climbing." Here was a boy who had been literally dealt a bad hand, yet he was so full of good nature and optimism that he infected an entire team. He was calm and sure of himself, and his unwavering belief in me helped me accomplish things I only dreamed of before. At that time, he was the only one I had met who had suffered through a divorce, but you couldn't tell it from talking to him. "Heck, I got friends all over the country now," he'd say. He changed my thinking about misfortune.

I lost a finger two years ago in a table saw accident. It was only my little finger on my left hand. I never thought much of it until it was gone, but I certainly have new respect for all of the work it performed while it was mine. I thought of Clay, and how he made do with what he had, laughed his southern laugh, and picked up his bat. Though I wasn't in the laughing mood much after losing my finger, I picked up my guitar, determined to play it as well if not better than I had before. And I did. It took months, but I could hear Clay telling me, "If you want it bad enough, you'll spend the time."

I'm thirty-six years old as I write this, and I marvel at the profound effect an eleven-year-old boy has had on my life. His complete comfort with who he was and what he had been given and his confidence in a new situation with a bunch of teasing youths — all of this showed me that real strength comes from what's inside of you, not in what others offer in passing jests. He held a mirror up to my soul and showed me what I could be, not what I was. His slow, steady grin greets me every time I call up his memory from the distant storage places in my mind. I may never see Clay again in my life, but his southern drawl is with me every day, chuckling at the petty jests and offering steady encouragement: "You'll git it...come on, jes' give it another try."

MY EVERYDAY HERO
By Jay Trenhaile

I had seen Ron Barthel around the weight room in the Field-house after I transferred to Dakota State University but had never had any interaction with him beyond a passing greeting. He was responsible for maintenance of the facility, and at that time in my life, weight training was usually a whole afternoon affair. My focus was always on working out not developing relationships with the staff.

Shortly after football practice started the following fall, how-ever, I started noticing Ron's positive relationship with upper classmen and the coaching staff. It seemed as if Ron knew all the athletes by name, and rarely did a player fail to question Ron about the fishing at Lake Madison or his plans for pheas-ant hunting. Obviously, Ron's caring, outgoing personality was appealing to my teammates.

That was the year that the fall football camp experienced con-sistent 100-degree temperatures. The weather was causing many of the first year players to seriously question their interest in continuing college football. However, after many three-a-day practices in scorching heat and the standard football initiation, fall camp, ended and it was time for our first game. A couple of nights before the first game, the senior player, for whom I was to perform various duties, informed me that I was to shine his football helmet and polish his shoes before the big game. I told the senior teammate that I had no polish or materials and could not comply with his request. He promptly directed me to Ron Barthel, who showed me to his office and located some polish. I suspect he had purchased these supplies himself to help athletes on such occasions. While getting started on the helmet and shoes, I noticed the starting quarterback, Mike, working on his helmet. The helmet was without marks; in fact, it looked as though Mike hadn't been at practice at all that fall. That made me wonder why in the world Mike would want to spend time on a relatively clean helmet. Meanwhile, I was becoming increasingly irritated at the work ahead of me. After I'd put forth a minimal effort on my "project," Ron questioned me about where *my* helmet and shoes were. Reluctantly, I retrieved my helmet and shoes and started polishing. While I worked, I listened to Ron as he started to talk about pride. He said things about taking pride in what one does and how it might be easy to quit caring about responsibilities, but that would affect one's self-image. He also discussed his work at the Fieldhouse and how he took pride in the cleanliness of the facility. These were messages like the "do your best" and "work hard" messages that I had heard before from my parents, teachers, and coaches, but something was different. This discussion had a significant effect on me. Although my first year of football was not what I had hoped, that discussion stuck with me. During the next season, I was ready to work harder and take pride in my responsibilities and, consequently, had more success.

That initial discussion was only one of many important interactions I had with Ron over the years. Ron always seemed available to help students out by listening to their concerns and giving them support in their activities. This support and availability came in spite of Ron's responsibilities to a family and another job. Another example of Ron's positive mentoring was his help with a friend of mine from Philadelphia, Mike T. It was late in the semester and nearing time for finals week. The pressure of finals and missing family and friends seemed to be wearing on Mike. He needed a stress release, and a workout seemed like a wise choice. Unfortunately the Fieldhouse was closed. However, after talking to Ron, Mike was able to arrange a workout through Ron. I was sure that the talk with Ron was as helpful as the workout itself or any other intervention available.

Ron was also well known for his fishing ability around Madison, SD and always had room in his boat for a student or two. He could often be found during days off teaching students how to fish. In fact, today, many graduates contact Ron and fish with him during their returns to the campus and community. A few years ago when I wanted to try ice fishing for the first time, I made one call and Ron answered that call.

One of the joys I have had in recent years has been to take my son, Thayer, to activities in Madison. Thayer has gotten to know Ron and looks forward to seeing him during our trips. One of Thayer's first trips ever to Madison was to attend a Dakota State Homecoming one fall. Thayer was barely old enough to walk, but when it came time for the parade, Ron had Thayer in the front row retrieving candy. Almost everybody passing out candy in the parade knew Ron, so Thayer ended up having more candy than any kid in attendance. When we go to Madison now, Thayer is always quick to ask about Ron's whereabouts. I simply reply that Ron is probably talking to someone because he has a lot of friends.

Clearly, Ron is an everyday hero. He is a person of passion, commitment, dedication, and morality. He takes pride in whatever he does, whether it is a job requirement, a leisure activity, or spending time with family and friends. For 17 years I have known and learned from Ron. He is the kind of person I want my children to emulate. Recently, I was pleased to learn that he is working with children in a preschool setting. The agency could not ask for a more dedicated, positive influence on our children.

MY EVERYDAY HERO
By Bill Tesch

Some memories never fade. Psychologists tell us that we have our emotions to thank for that. Intense anger, overwhelming lust, crushing sadness — every strong feeling seems to have the power to burn itself into our brains so that, at some future date, the mere smell of a brand of cigarettes or the sound of screeching brakes, or the tactile quality of a particular kind of cloth, will forever evoke in us one particular memory. Apparently, fear and helplessness have an especially powerful effect.

I guess I have fear and helplessness to thank for the fact that the otherwise delightful play of gently falling snow at sunset coupled with the annoying ring of my cellular phone will always take me back to the first Friday of December in 1998. I was just turning a corner in my pickup on my way to meet friends for dinner. Fat snowflakes slopped onto my windshield. This was the kind of snow that was often the precursor to big Midwestern storms. It was gratifying to turn on my windshield wipers and at once wipe away the residue of a week of dried-on road salt.

And so my mind was consumed with small thoughts and simple pleasures when the cellular phone rang. It was my wife. Chris was alone on the road to her annual get-together up in the Twin Cities with her sisters and her mother (no men allowed). The plan involved a four-hour drive followed by a rendezvous at a hotel in Minneapolis. The success of the plan depended upon three factors: a reliable vehicle, decent weather, and a little common sense. We did our part to insure success by getting the '88 Oldsmobile) into the shop for an oil change, tire rotation, flush and fill, and a 4761 point inspection . When the trip began under sunny skies about an hour and half before Chris called, it appeared that the weather would do its part as well. As far as common sense goes, Chris was about as expert as a layperson can be when it comes to travel and navigation — skills acquired while bailing me out of many a wrong turn and misread highway sign.

Something in the tone of Chris' voice caused me to do something that I should always do when talking on the phone while driving but that, admittedly, I have never done before or since, which was to pull over to the side of the road. As our conversation began, three disheartening observations immediately forced themselves upon me. First, the sudden and absolute onset of darkness. The sun had only just now set, yet taking its place was a starless, moonless, and completely overcast sky. Secondly, the sudden and startling onset of a raging winter storm. Those fat, wet flakes had multiplied and were now being propelled by a stiff northeastern wind. Finally, the barely-controlled panic in Chris' voice.

"Chris? Where are you?"

"I don't know."

At this moment I heard the unmistakable sound of my cellular phone losing its signal from the tower two blocks away. (Needless to say, the cellular phone company will not be appearing on my list of everyday heroes any time soon.) After a few agonizing minutes relearning how to adjust the call settings on my phone and getting the thing tuned into another tower, I was finally able to reestablish my connection to Chris' cellular.

"What's happened?" I asked.

"The car just stopped, it just died, it won't start, it just won't do anything at all. I keep turning the key and turning the key and it just...nothing happens...uhh, this car!"

"Well, where are you?"

"I don't know. I wasn't really paying attention to the signs. I know I'm a really long way from the turn-off, really long, but I don't know. I just don't know where I am."

"So you're, what, about half way between here and Rochester?"

"Maybe, I don't know. I just don't know, and I can't see anything. It got so dark all of a sudden, and now...it's a storm, a bad storm. When I turn the lights on, I can't see anything."

"Are you off the highway?" I asked inanely.

"Well, yes, I'm off the highway, of course I'm off the highway. Do you think I would just stop the car in the middle of the highway?"

"Sorry. Well, let's try this. Why don't we hang up and you can dial 911 and get emergency services in the area and then call me right back. Okay?"

"Does that work?"

"It's supposed to."

As I waited to hear back from Chris, I began to think. Thinking at a time like this is very bad. But there I was, envisioning my wife out there, and all the horrible things that could happen to her.

What if? What if someone, say a man, knocks on her window with a helpful smile on his face. What if his intentions are not honorable? I tried to imagine the kind of shiftless-humanity that might ooze out of small towns on nights like this in search of a little sport. How enticing would a young attractive woman be? It didn't help that Chris and I had just rented "Fargo."

I shook these thoughts aside and quickly replaced them with more realistic fears.

What if? What if it took all night to find Chris? I concluded that this was a realistic fear. Anyone searching for her would have to drive right up close to her vehicle in order to see it. There was zero visibility, and traffic would be moving at top speeds of 25-30 miles an hour. With the way this storm was shaping up, it was even possible that they would soon close the interstate. Her car would not start, which meant that the heater would not work, and as the storm grew stronger, the temperature inside the vehicle would grow colder. I began to feel a sense of panic, of urgency. My first thought was to start driving in that direction. I'd just go the 70? — 90? — 110? — 150? miles until I found her. But how far was it? And what if I didn't find her after 100 miles? Would that be the time to turn back and search again? Or should I go further? I thought,

"If this is how I'm feeling, what's Chris feeling right now?" I waited for her call.

"Nothing happens when I call 911."

"Nothing?"

"Nothing."

"What do you mean by 'nothing?'"

"I mean nothing, no ring, no sound, no nothing."

(I feel obliged to interject that the 911 feature was an especially strong selling point for these cellular phones.)

After a short silence, Chris began, "I just don't know what to do, can you come and get me?" This last statement was uttered in the form of a desperate plea.

"Yes I can, but I really want to find someone who can get to you sooner than I can."

"I know, I know."

While this was probably not all that helpful, my great fear and helplessness conspired to make me add these words to our exchange: "By the way, Chrissie, if anyone does stop to help you, keep your door locked, and just roll your window down a little crack to talk to them, you know, until you're,...you know...sure. You understand?"

"OK...yeah. I know, OK...But what should we DO?"

Chris had the idea of calling directory assistance and getting the number of a local sheriff's office. The only flaw in that plan was that neither of us knew which sheriff's office was, in fact, "local." I could just hear the conversation:

"Where is the vehicle located ma'am?"

"Somewhere in southern Minnesota."

We guessed that Albert Lea would hold the most promise, so we hung up while Chris made the call.

Several minutes later she called me back. She did not sound relieved or encouraged. "They said that they were pretty busy and since there was no way to be sure that I was in their county, they would pass it along to the Highway Patrol office." After a painful silence she added, "It's cold in here."

I asked, hopefully, "Can you at least get the engine running?" "No, I've tried so much I'm wearing down the battery. I don't want to try it any more, because if the battery dies I can't turn on my lights."

"Good thinking."

We decided to hang up so she could conserve her cellular battery and agreed to call every half hour. I realized that I was now already an hour and a half late to meet my friends for dinner and to pick up my kids. With a sudden pang of guilt, I proceeded on through the weather to the restaurant, while Chris waited alone somewhere in the darkness.

Officer Matt was a 15-year veteran of the Minnesota Highway Patrol. It was Officer Matt who got the call relayed to him from the Albert Lea Sheriff's office about a motorist stranded somewhere between Worthington and Albert Lea. The motorist was a lone young woman, driving a blue Oldsmobile. His first thought was that it would be a lot of miles to cover, and in this weather, that could mean a long night. We were to become grateful for many things that Officer Matt was to do later that evening, but as I think about him, I guess I am most grateful for a few small things that he did NOT do after receiving the call about Chris. He did not consider it someone else's job to find her. He did not think it a small thing for a young woman to be stranded on a night like this. He did not reason that his job was really law enforcement and that this matter, while important, would need to be relegated to the more important job of catching criminals and speeders. He did not hesitate. He did not think that it was a "car" that was stranded along the interstate but perceived that he was being called upon to assist a person.

We make these tiny decisions every day, every moment, in the course of our jobs. To make our demanding jobs easier, we sift through the work and decide "What is my work?" We do our best when go about our work knowing that there is a person out there who we need to serve. The heroes among us are the not-so-rare but still precious gems who are willing to do whatever it takes and to go above and beyond to serve that person out there.

Officer Matt began driving East about 20 miles west of Albert Lea. It was slow, methodical work, made more difficult because of the fact that at many places along the interstate, the opposite lane of traffic (where Chris would be) was either blocked by trees or, because of the weather, not even visible from Officer Matt's vehicle. If he happened to drive by the vehicle without seeing it, that mistake would prolong his search by several hours. Officer Matt had to be able to see every foot of the shoulder of the road in order to be sure not to miss Chris. It was likely that Officer Matt had to occasionally cross the median or even leave his vehicle to gain a proper view of the opposite lane.

A half hour later I was at the restaurant with friends, feeling warm, guilty, helpless, and afraid. We spoke and tried to reassure the kids that "Mommy was fine." Chris called once, twice — an hour had passed. It was cold, but she was staying relatively comfortable. Still no sign of help.

Then 40 minutes passed, and I worried so I made the call this time.

"Hi!" Now a more welcome set of emotions was evident in her greeting.

"What's up?" I asked hopefully.

"Well I'm OK, I'm with the State Trooper, His name is Matt, Officer Matt."

"Excellent! So now what?"

"Officer Matt is taking me to Albert Lea. I'll have to make arrangements to have the car towed there. I'm thinking of renting a car from there. What do you think?"

"How's the weather?"

"It's a little better now; I can drive in this."

"Oh, Chris, I'm so glad that you're OK now."

"Yeah, it was a little scary there...that dumb car!"

Officer Matt was already looming large in my personal list of heroes at this point, but there's more. You would think that the State Trooper's job at that point was pretty simple. Get the young woman to a safe location, make sure she makes arrangement for the vehicle, and be on your way. I'm guessing that's what the manual says. Here's what Officer Matt did.

It turned out that Albert Lea did not have an agency that could rent a vehicle for the weekend. Officer Matt suggested Rochester, another 60 or so miles away. He offered to drive her there. In Rochester at the office of the rental agency, Officer Matt must have noticed how dismayed Chris looked when she learned the price of renting a car for the weekend. He had a suggestion. "Why not call your sisters, who are probably at the hotel by now, and probably worried about you?"

"Oh that's right! I need to call them!"

"Yes, and why not ask them to come and get you and to meet you at the Owatonna Exit?"

Chris, now in near disbelief, "Owatonna? That's like another hour away from here, isn't it?"

"It's OK, I'll drive you there."

And so it happened that Officer Matt drove Chris another hour to rendezvous with her sisters in Owatonna and watched as their car headed safely north to Minneapolis.

Three things I'll never forget. I'll never forget that disconcerting moment when Chris called with panic in her voice; I'll never forget the sound of relief in her voice when I phoned her after she was safely aboard Officer Matt's patrol car. And I'll never forget Officer Matt, an everyday hero.

MY EVERYDAY HERO
By Ann Lewis Henkin

I remember the long, hot drives east across Texas through the deep Southern states towards Florida. It was 1959, a time when the U.S. was embroiled in racial conflict and discrimination. Our excitement over this vacation was unaffected by others' prejudices or the searing temperatures on this typically humid and sticky summer day. Our boat-sized station wagon was carefully packed with clothes, snacks, games, diapers, and enough wet washcloths to sustain five children and two adults until evening. Of course, Lucy was along. She had agreed to share the responsibility of the children and to help my mother drive in return for a Florida vacation. Lucy was a large, middle-aged, African American woman who was nurturing, loving, and competent. She had become a part of our family long before I was born and was now like my mother's right hand. They depended on each other. We loved to climb onto her ample lap and get lost in the strong arms lovingly wrapped around us.

I remember my mom signaling time to break for lunch and Lucy parking the car alongside a small Southern restaurant. We were just barely inside when the hostess noticed Lucy. She and my mom spoke briefly before the hostess walked to the kitchen and returned shortly thereafter with a commercial-sized pickle jar under her arm. My mom took the jar, gathered us together again, and ushered us out the door. She loaded my brothers and sisters in the car while Lucy and I circled to the back of the restaurant and filled the jar with water from the outside tap. We headed down the highway, disgruntled and hungry. My mother's lesson was simple and direct; if Lucy was not welcome inside, we would not eat there. The acrid taste of "pickle water" has remained with me to this day.

The moral of this story was reiterated later that evening as we searched for a motel to accommodate our family. My mother would enter a motel lobby and provide the information necessary for a room, only to be rejected upon mention of Lucy. This was an exhausting process, but my mother was insistent and could not be deterred. She would not allow other people's fear or bigotry to separate us. As children, we expected no less. Now, as an adult, I realize what a courageous stance this was and how she defied typical Southern ways to teach us a powerful lesson.

I remember, as a young girl, sitting beside my mom, trying to pluck long-ago stories from her memory. Her bittersweet smiles, glistening eyes, and hearty laughs brought to life those precious recollections of days gone by. She filled me with memories of my father, who had died shortly after my birth and painted images of old friends and meaningful events. This was an important resurrection, a sorting-out of who we were and where we belonged.

I remember the traditions of the seasons — the warmth of gingerbread and hot cocoa during the holidays and the delight of peppermint ice cream after hours of racing through the sprinkler on steamy Texas afternoons. I remember my mother's presence as I prepared for my first date, her pride at all our graduations, and her way of checking in with each of us five children as we gathered around the dinner table. Those were the rituals that sustained us and that sustain me now.

I remember the snakes, the frogs, and horned toads that were stealthily caught and released. I remember the endless number of injured birds we found each spring, boarded in shoeboxes, fed with eye-droppers, and nursed back to flight. I remember the secret gully swing, the puppies we adopted from the roadway, and hiding from the babysitter high in the treetops. There was nothing to compare to the richness of this hands-on teaching.

I remember the summers, how we raced barefoot down the gravel road or through the backyard woods. Summers were a time to spend with far-away grandparents, cousins, and aunts. This was a chance to reconnect with distant family. Family was important, vital; my mother felt we needed to hear their stories, too.

I remember my chagrin when I grew-up, left home, and learned that in many situations, women took a secondary role to men. How utterly frustrating to see competent people not viewed as equals. How strange, how silly, how baffling to learn that responsible, intelligent people (some like my very own mother) might be considered less capable based solely on their gender.

This did not coincide with my childhood teachings. Everyone in my family was expected to help-out and be responsible at home, at school, in our community, and in relationships with others. All of us were expected to pitch-in, do chores, and perform roles that were not particularly fitting to or liked by either gender (we all hated them equally!) but that simply needed to be accomplished to keep our home functioning properly.

My mom taught us that we were not less than anyone else... nor better but certainly equal. Her lesson was challenging and seemed so right; sons and daughters should have opportunities to become teachers, doctors, nurses, homemakers, and bankers based on their intelligence, their capabilities, their responsible behavior, and their tenacity — not on their gender or color.

These are the teachings of an everyday hero. These are the everlasting memories of childhood steeped in encouragement, care, humor, strong values, and unfaltering love. These are mere samplings of a family that experienced the joys, disappointments, hopes, tragedies, and wonders of life. These are the bumps along the way that stoked a determination to succeed and made us stronger and, hopefully, wiser.

As I was growing up, I never considered my upbringing to be exceptional and certainly never gave a thought to the long-term effect of my mother's childrearing. Today, as an adult and a parent, I realize the tremendous energy and the amazing dedication and how the simplicity of her life lessons actually worked.

This is the woman who raised me and my brothers and sisters primarily by herself. This is the bright, beautiful, inquisitive, and productive woman in her eighties who continues to be a nurturing, wonderful mom. This is the woman who certainly did not choose to do all of this on her own, but given the circumstances, she did it and did it with love, humor, and determination. This is the woman who provided energy and courage that fueled such an exciting childhood journey and coaxed the best from each of us.

This is my mother, my inspiration, my hero. And this is her great gift...a profound and enduring legacy of love.

MY EVERYDAY HERO

By Lyn Collver

It had been a moving and traumatic twenty-four hours. Now I stood looking at the frail form in the hospital ICU bed. I had worked in a medical environment for years, but nothing could have prepared me for the sight of tubes and machines connected to this man lying motionless and staring before me. "Dad... Dad," I softly tried the word.

"I'm sorry, but your five minutes is up," said a firm, gentle voice. I started from my thoughts and turned to go, whispering a prayer for strength and healing for this once robust and healthy man. Glancing back, I sent up a silent cheer. "Go, Dad!"

As I returned to the waiting room, my mind wandered through the past twenty-four hours, recalling my fear when the surgery stretched to five, six, eight hours. Dad had finally emerged with a balloon pump breathing for him, and now I tried valiantly to focus on the few words of hope the doctors could offer us.

My thoughts returned again and again to the night before. In the dim light of the hospital room, my dad's husky voice had broken the silence abruptly. "I love you!" His words took me by surprise. I had never heard those words from him before, at least not directed at me. "I love you too — Dad." I couldn't recall when I had last used that word in his presence. Yet it felt so right, so good. I was for the moment both a child and a woman. I was a child encircled in the arms of those words I had so long wanted to hear, and I was a woman embracing this now-small frame in my arms and offering reassurance as his body shook with sobs. This was a new place for our relationship, a place of rest and even joy, and we took refuge there, savored the moment as long as we could.

The following nine days would be filled with uncertainty and cautious hope as my feisty Swedish father fought for his life. I had many hours in which to ponder in my heart the man who couldn't say "I love you" to his children yet had spoken his love loudly through every action. Who was he? How did he live his life? What legacy would he pass down to his children and grandchildren?

Elmer Nelson, the tenth of twelve children born to Swedish immigrants, was raised short on love and long on survival. His mother died when he was eight, and his father was a cruel, relentless taskmaster who drank too much and protected too little. The siblings learned early in life that in order to survive one must eat faster, think quicker, talk louder, and fight harder. "Tough as nails" truly described these country kids. No pansies in the bunch!

My dad, however, learned early in life that survival required even more of him. A speech impediment, stuttering, clouded his young life, and he endured cruel, incessant taunting from his siblings. The pain left emotional scars but also taught him empathy, and he used each bitter experience to become a better person. He found that sometimes actions could communicate more strongly than words. Cleaning up the vomit on his inebriated father and helping him into bed was a way to express things he could never have put into words. All the while he was growing into a sturdy, muscular five-foot-nine who could lift a car or win the coveted trophy at the local threshing bee — a giant, but a wounded giant.

His life became a showpiece of compassion and integrity, whether he was dealing with adults or little children. When I was only four years old, I snuggled in bed one night listening to the reassuring hum of voices in the kitchen. The door, open just a crack, revealed my dad and his friend Marshall at the kitchen table, drinking coffee and smoking cigarettes. Somehow, I feared those cigarettes intuitively. I sobbed out my fears and pled, "Please, Daddy, don't smoke. I don't want you to die!" That night, my dad vowed to a desperate little girl that he would never smoke again. He put a little girl's tears and fears before his own desires and kept that vow, proving that he was both a gentle man of compassion and a strong man of integrity. The lifelong trust that he always inspired in me began that very night.

His integrity was just as firm where money was concerned. I recall a time when my sister was sick and Dad had to borrow $100 from a family friend to pay the bill. Pride was put aside; family needs came first. But he wouldn't forget the debt, either. Every night he would sit by the kitchen table and rub his balding head, struggling with our meager finances. And every month he managed to send one dollar to that friend until the bill was paid. At the end of 96 weeks, we celebrated. Dad's character and integrity shone brightly that day.

Although we were quite poor, I never suspected it until I was eleven years old and we moved to the city. There we were transported into a magical land of running water, indoor toilets, light switches, basements, and garages. I didn't even have to sleep in the dining room on a lumpy cot anymore! I believe I owed my earlier lack of awareness to my parents' sense of values and to their indifference to the materialistic. I don't recall my dad ever being envious of others or speaking of what he didn't or couldn't have. Instead, I remember his willingness to share what we did have and to help someone less fortunate through a difficult time.

Dad was probably the least self-centered and most unselfish person I ever knew. He worked hard and gave much. Before we moved to the city, he always rose before dawn. I would hear the milk cans clang and clatter as he went about his mundane morning chores. The few cows he milked would greet him in the darkness. Sometimes, I would hear a muttered expletive as their friendly tails met the milk can in disaster. He would work long past dusk, relentlessly plowing the dusty, unyielding fields, hoping that his would be the year of the windfall crop. He was a tireless worker, persevering in spite of extreme adversity, self-disciplined to a fault. His unselfishness and hard work didn't mean much to me then. Now, I recall with amazement that he wore the same suit to church for many years — long after it ceased to fit properly! — so his little girls could have new crisp Easter bonnets and festive Christmas dresses. I also remember there were no gifts under the Christmas tree for him, but for us there was always a coveted doll or cuddly teddy bear.

His giving spirit and unselfishness were not orchestrated for the moment. They defined who he was and described how he lived. Many years later, he continued to work hard, spend little, and give much. Due to his sacrifices, a young mother of five was able to achieve a dream: getting an education. A graduate of eighth grade in a small country school, my dad believed in learning by experience and even made fun of educational pursuits. Yet he honored his youngest daughter's goal to be educated and made that distant dream a reality and I will be forever grateful.

But if my father knew the value of hard work and honesty, compassion and trust, he also knew the value of a good sense of humor. His hearty laughter echoed through the house as his stories grew in number, intensity, and enormity! He had the presence of a born tale-teller, the gift of making others laugh — and as was his way, he gave this gift freely with no expectations of getting a return on his investment. He was the one who greeted the unacceptable, spoke with the intolerable, hugged the unlovable. His was the smile that touched hearts and broke down defenses.

Yet this man who found it so easy to reach out to others closed the emotional door on his children. I never thought of his behavior as "abnormal" when I was growing up; oh, I occasionally envied friends whose fathers would hug and cuddle and say "I love you" without thought or effort. But I never spoke of it because I didn't know how to begin. I tried not to think of it because I didn't want to be different. Looking back, I realize that I had all the time what mere words can never give. I had evidence of love through self-sacrifice, through strong morals, through an unwavering sense of honor. This legacy will long be remembered, appreciated, and applauded. Dad, I thank you for loving me without words. And Dad, I also thank you for the gift of love through words that night a few years ago. I guess I always knew you loved me. I simply needed to hear you say it one time.

III. THE EVERYDAY HEROES OF UNIVERSITY STUDENTS

MY EVERYDAY HERO
By Stephanie Steichen

When one thinks of a hero, one thinks of an extraordinary person who goes above and beyond the call of duty to do the right thing. My hero is a person who has overcome great adversity in her life to become one of the strongest people I know. My friend, Ronda, is an example of someone who had every possible disadvantage and fought with all her might not to let life get her down — and succeeded.

Ronda and I became friends when we were in the third grade. Her family had moved into town from the country, and we spent a lot of time together playing games and being tomboys. I did not know what was going on with her family behind closed doors until I was a senior in high school. Perhaps when you are that young, you don't notice the signs or you ignore them.

By the time Ronda and I entered middle school, we were inseparable. We were always together, and I spent a lot of time at her house. Ronda's real dad had left before she was born, and her mother remarried a Vietnam Veteran who adopted Ronda. Her mother was very hard on Ronda. She obsessed about the house being clean and forced Ronda to do much of the work. If something wasn't done, it was Ronda's fault; if supper wasn't ready on time, it was Ronda's fault. Ronda's younger brother and sister were spoiled and had little responsibility. Ever since I can remember, her parents were constantly yelling at her in front of me and calling her names. She was often called a slut, which particularly upset me because she made a point of staying away from boys.

Later in life, Ronda told me that she used to be embarrassed sometimes when I would come over because her parents regularly smoked pot and who knows what else; and she was afraid I would smell the pot. I never recognized the smell for what it was. It was just a characteristic of their house.

By the time we entered high school, Ronda had already developed a reputation because of her family. In a small town, your last name can label you; this can be an advantage or a disadvantage. For Ronda, it was a disadvantage. She had to work harder than the rest of the class to prove herself. She was extremely smart and had to prove that to everyone by taking physics and calculus instead of study halls. She was a talented cheerleader and always had a smile on her face.

As I look back on the course of our friendship, the signs of verbal, physical, and sexual abuse seem obvious. I think I always knew deep down what was happening, but I was afraid to do or say anything. Ronda did miss a lot of school, and sometimes she would have bruises on her body. Only one time did she admit to me that her mother had hit her.

Her father was on heavy medication and spent a lot of time at the VA Hospital. Ronda sometimes mentioned how he would forget to take his medication and "flip-out."

Ronda's parents got divorced when we were seniors in high school, and Ronda moved into a small apartment with her dad because she couldn't get along with her mother. She was starting to get sick, and she looked really rundown and tired. I finally had to admit to myself that something was seriously wrong and that she needed help. I confronted Ronda about the living situation with her father, and she told me that she hadn't been able to sleep because she was afraid of him. That was all that she would tell me, but I went home and asked my parents if she could move in with us. They didn't hesitate to say yes, and that day we started moving her in.

Later that night, my dad received a phone call from the sheriff. Ronda's dad had taken her out into the country and put a gun to her head, threatening to kill her for leaving him. She miraculously escaped, and had gotten to the police. They had to search all night before they finally found her. I'll never forget how Ronda looked when I walked into the station and saw her sitting with her head in her hands crying uncontrollably. I had never seen my dad cry before, but he got tears in his eyes when she grabbed on to him and wouldn't let go. My parents had come to love her like a daughter over the years.

That was a scary night, and finally everyone had to face the truth about what was going on. The police convinced Ronda not to press charges because her father needed to go to a mental hospital and get treatment. After he was released from the hospital, he would call and harass her until she finally got a restraining order requiring him to leave the state. She was so scared, and I remember that I couldn't talk her into going to the senior prom. She stayed home and played games with my little sister.

Ronda told my mom everything that had happened to her while she was growing up. Her father had molested her since she was little, and she was physically and verbally abused by both her parents. She still has told me very little, and I have not pushed her. She had nightmares for a long time, and I'm sure she still does. I would just hold her and tell her everything would be OK.

Ronda is my hero because she has refused to give in to the low standards of her parents. She was told all of her life that she wasn't worth anything, that she was a slut and a whore and that she was stupid. She could have taken those comments to heart, but she did the opposite. She never took drugs or slept around. She excelled at school and sports. She held her head high, and she always smiled.

After we graduated, she met a really nice guy whom she later married. His dad walked her down the aisle. They now have two daughters, and I am amazed every time I see Ronda with her children. She is going to be the mother that she never had. She is so caring and so in love with her kids. She would never hurt them like her parents did her.

Ronda had always wanted to go to college, and I try to convince her that she still can, but for now she's content raising her family.

Somehow Ronda did more than survive all the tragedy in her life: she came out of it as a strong, beautiful person. She would do anything for anybody, and she doesn't like to see people get hurt. She learned from her experience and tries to help others feel worthy. She is smart and responsible, and she makes the right moral decisions. Ronda understandably doesn't trust very many people because she is afraid of getting hurt, but she wants others to trust her, and they can.

If all of us were like were like Ronda, we sure wouldn't complain as much as we do. She doesn't feel sorry for herself, and sometimes when I complain about something trivial I stop and think about how lucky I am and have been.

I still can't figure out where she got her spirit and her laugh. Sometimes she sends my family and me little cards just saying thank you. She is grateful to everyone who has helped her. Ronda is a true inspiration to me and has helped make me a better person. She shows that anyone can conquer adversity and succeed in life. She is genuinely an everyday hero!

MY EVERYDAY HEROES
By Teresa Delfinis

My lessons in life have often been learned as a result of facing adversity. The difficult decisions I have had to make were made easier with the feedback, support, and encouragement of those closest to me.

As a child, I grew up on my paternal grandparents' farm in rural South Dakota. My parents lived in a house on this same farm in order to share the responsibilities involved in the farm's operation. Although this was probably not an ideal situation for my parents, I benefited greatly from my relationship with my grandparents. They taught me much about life in general and instilled many of the values that are still important to me today.

My parents had married at an early age because of an unplanned pregnancy. My father had only completed the eighth grade by the time he quit school to work full-time on the farm, and my mother dropped out of school at the age of sixteen to become a wife and mother. As a result, my parents didn't place a high priority on education.

However, my grandparents did believe that education was important, and it could open the door to many opportunities. Because of their influence, I did very well in school and graduated at the top of my senior high class. I did not enter college, however, for financial reasons. I decided to work for a year in order to save money, with the goal of entering college the next fall.

During this time period, I met the man who would eventually become my husband. However, there would be no fairy-tale ending at this point in time. I became pregnant with my daughter at the age of nineteen. Her father wasn't ready for the responsibility of a child and wanted nothing to do with the situation. My choices were to have an abortion, give my child up for adoption, or keep my child and raise her on my own. With the support and council of my grandparents, I made the decision to go through with the pregnancy and raise my daughter by myself.

My newborn daughter became the most important positive influence in my life. I had always had doubts about my abilities; a little voice inside my head had always told me I would never be able to accomplish the things I wanted to. My daughter's birth changed this. I knew I was responsible not only for my own destiny but hers as well.

As a result, I gained the confidence to go after life and get the things out of it that I wanted. I'm not saying that I didn't encounter setbacks, but the good far outweighed the bad, and I became a much nicer person to be around. I no longer blamed others for things that happened in my life but took responsibility for my own actions.

Because of the changes in me, my child's father became more interested in spending time with our daughter. We also grew closer, and when our daughter was three, we decided to get married. I now realize that if we had gotten married because of the pregnancy, we would not be together now. We both needed time to grow and find answers to questions in our lives.

Pursuing an education was still an important goal. However, we were not financially secure enough for me to go to school. Instead, we both worked in order to save money so that eventually I would be able to fulfill my dream of obtaining an undergraduate degree. Years passed without any hope of taking classes because something always took priority over education. However, life has a way of making one reevaluate. At the age of thirty-two, I nearly died as a result of blood clots in my lung and leg. I came within a few hours of losing my leg. The battle back was long and hard, but with the help from my family and God, I made it.

During my recuperation, I thought often about my desire to go to school. I had always put it off for another day. However, I now knew from personal experience that tomorrow might never come. As a result, I discussed the possibility of enrolling in classes with my husband and daughter. They were both very supportive of the idea and encouraged me to go for it. However, the little voice inside myself resurfaced and made me doubt my ability to succeed.

Because my father-in-law placed such a high value on education, he encouraged me to continue on and pursue a college degree. As a young man, he had received a degree in electrical engineering. Later on in his life, he decided to go back to school to pursue another degree in mechanical engineering in order to better provide for his family. In addition, he loved learning for the pure joy of it.

Because my father-in-law knew what it was like to work on a degree as a non-traditional student, his advice and suggestions carried a lot of weight. He was very proud of me and always encouraged me to do my best. In fact, my father-in-law often told my husband that he saw the potential that was hidden in me, just waiting to be discovered. He called me a "a diamond in the rough." Unfortunately, my father-in-law died shortly after I obtained my undergraduate degree. His legacy and spirit, however, will live with me forever.

As a result of the support of my husband, daughter, and father-in-law, I decided to take a couple of classes and see how it went. How could anyone have predicted how well it would go? Because of my success, I was motivated to continue on, and eventually I quit my job to pursue my education full-time. In May of 1997, I graduated from South Dakota State University with highest honors.

Although the negative little voice inside myself occasionally resurfaces, it isn't nearly as loud as it used to be because of my accomplishments. My belief in my own abilities has continuously been fed by the unwavering support of my husband and daughter. I have learned, by venturing from my comfort zone, that I am capable of succeeding at anything I set my mind to.

In addition, I now know that no matter what path I choose to travel in life, those closest to me will be there to help guide and encourage me along the way.

MY EVERYDAY HERO
By Sharon Ramorski

An everyday hero is often overlooked. When we think about heroes, most of us probably think first of a famous singer, sports player, or actor — just as I did. But with more reflection I realized that my everyday hero is someone I speak to nearly everyday. I am privileged to have my mother as my everyday hero. There are many reasons why my mom meets the requirements of an everyday hero. If you met her walking on the street, in a coffee shop, at church, or as your nurse in the recovery room, you would recognize that she has something very unique: a gift of love for everyone.

As a little girl, I watched intently as my mom went about her day. I would imagine I was just like her as I played house in my bright yellow playroom. At times, my mom would join me, but mostly she would poke her head in from time to time and give me a smile of reassurance and comfort.

Often we would meet my grandmother for lunch, and the three of us would head into town for shopping. I could listen for hours to their conversations. They would always include me and ask what I thought. They respected my ideas, which I'm quite sure were often long-winded and made no sense. My mom always made me feel as if I belonged.

Soon I was old enough for school. I remember hesitantly climbing the big steps of Bus 15 on my first day of school. Mom was outside taking snapshots and waving and yelling that she would meet me at the school to take me to my room. And once I got to school, there she stood, just as she had promised. I recall hanging onto her hand shyly as we walked into the classroom. I could feel her love, encouragement, and confidence surround me even as she nudged me gently to go and play with my new friends. This first-day ritual continued until about the third grade — when I finally had the confidence to know that everything would be all right.

Mom's work involved much more than the first days of school. We had numerous tension-filled trips to the dentist, waiting to learn if I had cavities or would have to face the novocaine needle. Not only is my mom a nurse outside the home but an angel of mercy at home as well. My first cut that actually drew blood, late night fevers, and my bouts of ear infections kept her nursing skills honed.

She encouraged responsibility by listening to me practice the piano and try to make some sort of sound out of my flute. She would clap at my attempts and sing to the songs I proudly pounded out on the keyboard. She always told me that I needed to put forth my best efforts and strive towards growth in everything I did.

I also consider my mom a hero because of her walk with Christ. She has always stressed the importance of prayer and its powerful effect. She serves the Lord in many ways, from teaching religious education classes and attending daily mass to delivering Meals on Wheels to the elderly. She never complains during her delivery rounds and always takes the time to give a cheerful — but never patronizing — greeting to every person who opens his or her door for food. Her example of grace, service, and gratitude has truly brought me into a life of full surrender to God.

As a nurse, my mom demonstrates respect and caring towards her patients as she tries to ease their pain. Her pleasure in serving others in this way is evident in the passion with which she carries out her work. By tolerating and embracing differences, whether with her patients or co-workers, she also brings out the best in others.

As I approached my teen years, I didn't think I needed my mom so much anymore and certainly wasn't going to confide in her. Oh, she was there to teach me how to drive and be the occasional shopping partner, but I depended less and less on her. She in turn allowed me to test my wings.

By the time I turned 18, I required her undivided attention once again as I battled with an eating disorder and struggled for survival. It was my mom who spent months feeding her high school senior as if she were an infant. She would lie next to me as I slept, watching my stomach move up and down and listening for my next breath. She would pray that I would make it through the night, and in the morning, she would start feeding me and providing unconditional love all over again. She ultimately put her career on hold to drive me two hours for therapy twice a week. When I no longer had the strength or courage to fight for my life, my mom had the resilience and determination to sustain me. My mom would often say that "God never gives you anything you can't handle," yet I believe she was truly trying to convince herself at times. Throughout it all, she never swayed from her mission to heal, love, and pray. Her strength, courage, and compassion was a torch for me to follow throughout my illness. I eventually overcame my eating disorder and have become a better person for it. But if not for the mother who believed in me, I would not be here today. As Marion Garrett stated, "A mother's love is the fuel that enables a normal human being to do the impossible." I can now view the impossible as possible and appreciate that life and love are the greatest of all gifts.

My mother demonstrates the pillars of life: respect, trustworthiness, caring, responsibility, fairness, and citizenship. She is a true role model in all of these areas yet is humble in her walk through life. She is not perfect; no one is. Yet she consistently exhibits good character and ethical behavior no matter what the situation. She knows that only she can be held accountable for her actions, so she pursues life with care — confident that her rewards will be great in heaven. I will always deeply believe in the power and beauty and heroism of my mother's love. I owe all that I am or hope to be to my mother — my hero.

MY EVERYDAY HERO
By Susan Negstad

My first impressions of Rob come from my days as a high school substitute teacher. It is very difficult for substitutes to know the daily routine of the classes they teach. Furthermore, substitute teachers can become the easy target of torture by uncaring students. But I was fortunate to meet Rob, an unusually mature student. He would go out of his way to explain the procedures that his high school usually followed and ensure my experience was pleasant. I always double-checked the information he gave me, but everything Rob told me was exactly correct. It was enormously helpful to have found a student I could trust.

During the school year, the elementary students were presented with the D.A.R.E. program. The principal asked for seniors willing to speak with the children who were in the program. When he asked for volunteers, he made a specific requirement: any students who volunteered had to be able to look the elementary students in the eye and say honestly that they did not drink, smoke, or use any other drugs that were illegal. Rob was only one of two who could volunteer his time and who could make that claim.

I eventually learned where Rob got his moral values and the courage of his convictions. Rob's family was a very close one. His parents came to all his sporting events along with his older brother, who took time off from college to attend his brother's events. I spoke with Rob's mother at prom while we were both chaperoning. She mentioned at one point that she had taught her kids to practice abstinence. While so many parents hope that their children will practice abstinence, few actually make it a family expectation and demand compliance. I could tell Rob had come from a strong family that cared enough to set high moral standards.

During the summer of 1999, I took a graduate course on Grief Counseling and interviewed Rob for a class assignment. As a junior, Rob had lost a friend who committed suicide. When Rob came in for the interview, I explained what I needed for the paper and how involved he would be personally. I also told him who would be reading the paper. He was very willing to help in spite of the pain it would entail.

We began talking. He discussed his relationship with his deceased friend and told me about the details of his suicide. As he spoke about the different events that surrounded the suicide, he worked through a lot of pain but remained very open. During the conversation, we both shared how we have been affected by deaths in our lives and discussed our reactions to death.

During our conversation, many other topics came up. We discussed alcohol consumption. Rob said he did not drink alcohol. He said that other students who had not been drinkers or at least had not been heavy drinkers often started drinking around graduation time. He himself was *not* going to start. He was aware that he may have been a little less popular socially due to his stand on drinking, but Rob was a strong individual and would not compromise his values because of peer pressure.

Last spring, I was the director of the all-school play, and Rob's girlfriend, Cassie, was the female lead character. In the play, the lead female and the lead male were to kiss. Cassie had told me that Rob was a little upset about the kiss. The male lead had been teasing Rob about it. I explained the scene to Rob and said that the kiss needed to stay in the play, that it was nothing more than a kiss. While he still was not comfortable with the scene, Rob was more understanding and not as upset by the situation. He was even willing to videotape one of the three productions because he was so proud of his girlfriend. He showed an unusual maturity in accepting the situation that many adults do not even show.

Rob is a very dedicated student and is especially adept in dealing with computers. During the summer, I was having problems with my personal laptop computer. I had tried to shut it down but could not get it to shut down no matter what I tried. The computer had been on for a few hours and was getting hot. I began calling people. The people I tried to contact who knew a lot about computers were not available. I happened to have Rob's number from when I interviewed him, so I finally called him. Rob talked me through different steps, and eventually we got the problem solved. Never once was he condescending about my lack of computer knowledge!

Rob is one of my "everyday heroes" for many reasons. He is eighteen years old and has many wonderful qualities that some adults never acquire. He is intelligent and kind, quick-witted and compassionate, knowledgeable and empathetic. He has strong convictions and a mature outlook. He is a true "everyday hero" who demonstrates impressive moral courage.

MY EVERYDAY HERO
By James Green

I have been very fortunate to be married to an "everyday hero" for more than twenty-two years. When I first met my wife Marilyn, we were both college students. Over the years we have both learned from one another, but I believe I have learned a great deal more from her. She is a person of great character and courage, qualities that she exhibits every day and qualities that she has taught me to believe in and develop.

Marilyn has great personal strength and fortitude. She was born with very severe scoliosis; the curvature of her spine is 85% of what it should be. To a person born in the 1950's, there was no miracle surgery available. She began first grade wearing a full-body plaster cast from just below her shoulders to just above her hips. Even at this young age, she saw the need to take responsibility for her personal growth and development by always looking for opportunities to help others. She struggled with the biannual changing of the cast and the general discomfort of wearing it. She would wear the cast until her senior year in high school.

The average person would have given up; Marilyn charged ahead. She concentrated on activities and academics. She graduated from the eighth grade from the rural school she was attending and began her freshman year at Elk Point High School. Within a few weeks, she later told me, she figured that she could handle this bigger school and that she was as smart as these kids, so she set out to prove it. Prove it she did. She graduated number one in her class. She also participated in girl's athletics, pom-pom girls and other activities. She also attended prom. She did all this while still wearing the plaster cast.

Marilyn graduated from college and taught business education at a high school for three years. During her third year she decided to leave the education field and seek a job in business. She began work on a Master's of Business Administration. A job in business was not easy to come by with a tight labor market, but her belief in herself and her personal integrity helped her to find a position with a large bank. She has now worked for the bank for 19 years.

A test of Marilyn's character came in 1995 when she was diagnosed with breast cancer. She could easily have reacted with anger at the world, God, the doctors, and anyone associated with the disease or its treatment. Instead, she trusted her cancer doctor. As she went through chemotherapy, she maintained a positive outlook. She told me once, "This is just something we have to get through." Her plan was to attack with personal strength and not back down. During this time, she was empowering and encouraging others with the attitude that things would be all right, that we would get through this.

Since her recovery, she has continued to remain a person of great character and heroism. A number of people close to us have had to battle cancer in the past few years. She has been a trusted friend to each and every one of them. She seeks to help them see the positives during their battles with illness. She gives freely of her time and attention. She stands by them when they lose their hair during chemotherapy, an event that is especially difficult for some people. When she met a woman at the Mayo Clinic who could not afford a wig or turbans, she donated hers.

When her closest friend came down with cancer, Marilyn was with her throughout the ordeal. She has called friends of friends and co-workers' family members who were fighting cancer to offer support and encouragement. She has been supportive to their family members as well.

Perhaps the best demonstration of Marilyn's character was when her cousin's son, Jeremy, was diagnosed with bone cancer. Marilyn took the diagnosis very hard initially. Then, true to her nature, she collected herself and started doing what she could to be supportive of Jeremy and his family. She called them frequently. She made special trips to see them. She brought Jeremy gifts and offered words of encouragement to the family.

I believe that she gave them the strength to fight the battle. She understood, first as a survivor herself and also as a mother. Unfortunately, Jeremy lost the battle and died recently. While Marilyn grieved, she also continued to be supportive of his family and her own. She was empathetic towards their grief and understanding of their loss. She made sure that her cousin had the time and the support she needed to deal with the loss.

Marilyn will always remain my "everyday hero." When I am at my lowest, she is there with a sympathetic ear. Her love, understanding, and support have continued throughout the years of our marriage. And whatever situation life puts her in, she continues to reach for the stars.

MY EVERYDAY HEROES
By Dianne Nester

Individuals touch our lives in many unique and different ways. Some people come into our lives to teach us lessons about life, and some people even guide us over the stumbling blocks and onto the path of greater fulfillment. We are blessed when friendships and relationships are formed in which acceptance, courage, honesty, hope, and love are evident. My everyday heroes are those helping professionals who encouraged me to be the woman I am today and experience fullness of life.

Pastor Anne motivated me to take an important first step in accepting problems in my life. Several years ago, I realized I was not truly living life each day; I was merely surviving. My husband was emotionally, physically, and sexually abusing me. I feared his touch. I was constantly afraid because I didn't know when he might go into another rage. In addition, he drank a six-pack of beer or more daily. For all of these reasons, I had become very depressed. Ambivalent feelings took over my life. I was contemplating leaving my husband and trying to determine if he was an alcoholic. I wondered what was wrong with me because I felt like I could no longer handle the daily drinking and rages.

When the chaos finally overwhelmed me, I decided to talk with my pastor. As I poured out my confusion, fear, pain, and sorrow, she listened. Pastor Anne asked me if I thought that God intended for me to live like this and assured me God did not. Eventually, I confronted my husband's drinking and uncontrolled anger. When my husband joined an outpatient treatment program for alcoholism, I started working with a counselor to deal with my own issues.

My counselor, Jane, inspired me to have the courage to face unresolved issues in my life. By now, my husband had stopped drinking, and our daughters and I returned home. But while my husband had attended out-patient treatment for alcoholism, he did not acknowledge he had an alcohol problem. He told me, "I used to drink the same amount that my friends did. I am not an alcoholic and don't you ever say that I am." I was confused by this. While I was trying to face the truth in my life, he was distorting it. His anger and rages continued and even worsened. Now that he wasn't drinking, he was developing other addictions to replace his daily alcohol consumption. I struggled with the question of leaving or staying in my marriage. Jane told me, "Your pain will be much greater before it is better. When the pain of staying is greater than the pain of leaving, you will leave."

Jane and I worked on defining my fears, and I realized that my fear of the unknown was a major stumbling block for me. I could not imagine myself being divorced after twenty-two years of marriage. If I left my husband, surely I would fall apart or go crazy. It took me a couple of years to get enough courage to separate and file for a divorce. It was not easy going through the divorce process, but I survived. After the divorce, a great burden was lifted from me, and I discovered peace and meaning in my life. Today, I know it is okay to be divorced; I am not a complete failure, and I am a stronger person for having gone through the experience. With Jane's help, I found the courage to move on with my life in spite of my fears.

I was encouraged by both Anne and Jane to go back to school. The message was, "Go after your dream of being a counselor. I know you can make a difference in the lives of those who are depressed, grieving, and involved in addictions." Once I was back in school, many of my instructors inspired me further. They not only told it like it was; they lived what they taught. They modeled their self-confidence and their love of their work. I was especially awed to meet males who were sincere, calm, even-tempered, loving, and warm individuals. Going back to school helped me grow and gain self-confidence; I have an enthusiasm for education and personal growth that is stronger than ever. I believe learning is a life-long process that I will always desire.

Lori, the facilitator of a group called "Rebuilding When Your Relationship Ends," also became an everyday hero to me. By modeling her humanness, she taught me that I didn't have to be a robot or a Barbie doll; I could be a flesh-and-blood human being. I learned that part of being human is accepting the fact that we will make mistakes, but we can learn from them and move forward. I saw firsthand that there were others from all walks of life who had also gone through a divorce. Lori and the group showed me that I was not alone. I volunteered as a helper for the next "Rebuilding" group. The personal growth that the other members of the group and I experienced was truly amazing as the ten three-hour sessions passed by quickly. It was of such benefit to talk with others who had experienced similar circumstances. I took charge of my life. I am no longer a "doormat" for my ex-husband to walk all over. I developed boundaries with others, and I am working on enforcing them. I am a worthy individual who has needs and wants. I am a valuable person who lives and loves life instead of simply surviving.

I am not running from life now that I have the courage to face my past. I am willing to look at what is inside of me and do the work to accomplish my goal of freedom, living a much happier and more peaceful existence.

I am coming to terms with the truth that I have been emotionally, physically, and sexually abused in the past. As I face these demons, I do what I need to do to get through the darkest days by journaling, crying, praying, walking, listening to music, or calling a friend. I was ashamed to the core of my very being, but I am determined to move on with my life. I pray to God for guidance and for the strength to do the work I need to do in order to heal. I am going to walk away a stronger person because I am a survivor. I am no longer a victim.

The helping professionals that saved my life from emotional ruin have become everyday heroes to me and have encouraged me to take ownership of my life. I have been told by others that I am a completely different woman today from the one I was several years ago. Life is too short to pass each day merely trying to survive in misery. I am very thankful for the people in my life who have given me the courage, hope, and love that inspired my personal growth.

MY EVERYDAY HERO
By Tricia Harrod

I am lying in bed, the darkness swirling around me. It is late, and I am tired, but I cannot sleep. I need help. There is something on my mind, and I don't know what to do. Or maybe more truthfully, I don't have the courage to do what I know is right. I close my eyes and imagine her. Beautiful sparkling, blue eyes; soft gray hair; plump arms covered with age spots that welcome me into a nice warm cushy lap. I lean my head on her chest and hear the steady beat of a heart that loves me. As she holds me I ask, "What should I do? Am I strong enough to make the right decision?" No sooner do I ask than I feel strength entering my body. Just her presence, although only in my mind, is enough to prod me in the right direction and give me the courage to act accordingly. As I start to relax and breathe deeply, she slowly fades from my memory. I am no longer restless and tortured. I now have the courage to do what I know is right. I drift into a comfortable dream state with a sense of relief that only comes from absolute peace.

She always knew the right thing to do or say and the respectable way to behave. It was not a show but something deeper. It was a regard for others and for life that conducted my grandmother's way through the world. She didn't preach good character; she exuded it. Everyone around her knew they were with someone special. Faces would light up upon her arrival. Her respect for human beings showed in her refusal to talk badly about other people. She did not gossip nor did she encourage gossip from those she encountered. I do not remember ever hearing her say anything negative about another. Grandma treated those around her just as she expected to be treated, with respect and fairness.

As a young girl I occasionally got to spend a couple of nights with Grandma. As soon as I would get into the house I would run to the kitchen and wait beneath the old white-painted cabinets. I stood there excitedly hoping Grandma would remember my favorite treat. I loved peanut butter and would watch as Grandma picked out a spoon, sometimes teasing me by pretending to choose a small one. She would dip the spoon into the peanut butter, fill it full, and then place it into my greedy fist. I would slowly savor each lick on the spoon, not wanting the tasty glob to disappear.

This whole ritual was very special to me. One night I tried to sneak a second spoon without asking. Grandma gently scolded me, "I said only one spoon. You should have asked if you wanted another. Because you disobeyed and tried to deceive me, you cannot have any tomorrow night."

As a child and even into my adolescent years, I expected Grandma to put fair limits on me and enforce consequences for pushing those limits. The consequences were never severe, but the hardest part was knowing I had violated Grandma's trust in me to do the right thing.

Grandma not only expected to be able to trust me but was also very trustworthy herself. I knew when I asked her something that she was going to be honest in her answer. I could trust that what she was saying was exactly how she felt. She would not sugarcoat her answer nor give the popular one. Her answer would be honestly stated in a kind, caring way. Grandma would also be very discreet with what I told her. Often her response was, "I'll keep it under my hat." I always knew my secret was safe with her.

Grandma took responsibility for what her actions said to others. For example, she believed that any television program or movie that was not fit for children was not fit for her either. It did not matter if the show was right in the middle of the most exciting scene; if it were immoral, she would shut it off. We would ask, "Grandma, can't we watch that?" She would respond, "No, let's play a game instead." Even though we were not allowed to finish the show, the fun did not stop because Grandma would get us fully engaged in the game, and we soon forgot about the program. She taught us that just because you were an adult did not mean you were protected from being impacted by what you viewed on television.

Grandma grew up in poverty and lived the hard, humble life of a farmer's wife. Grandma and Grandpa saved their pennies for their children, never putting their own needs first. Grandma would eat the gizzard and neck of the chicken, convincing her children that she liked those pieces. Years later my mother discovered Grandma did not find the gizzard and neck tasty but ate them so her family could have the better pieces. In the same generous, caring spirit, Grandma sent several of her grandchildren on an overseas religious retreat using her inheritance from a deceased brother. She did this to enrich the moral character of her descendants. She truly believed that you reap what you sow. For her, there was no better way to spend the money than to give her grandchildren an incredible opportunity to grow.

You could not separate Grandma from her character; they were intertwined. Good character was not a mask she put on and removed. It was a part of her soul. Many years of being true to what she believed made her as strong as steel and as loving as a child. It was not uncommon for her to challenge people twice as big and much more powerful if they were advocating something that violated good character. Though Grandma never believed even for a moment that she was better than anyone else, she saw it as her duty to help keep the world's character climate clean. Grandma was led by an unshakable belief in God and lived her life according to the Golden Rule. She expected nothing less in those around her. She made trustworthiness, respect, responsibility, fairness, caring, and citizenship her way of life. It was not just a catchphrase but the foundation of her principles.

As you can see, Grandma has had such an incredible impact on my life. When I am faced with a moral dilemma, I ask myself, "What would Grandma do?" At other times when I am leaning towards taking the low road, my conscience will protest, "Is that something you would be proud to tell Grandma you did?" It is pretty hard to justify the "wrong" choice with her "watching." She is my personal character guide, a lighthouse pointing me through the murkiness of ethical and moral issues. Even though she no longer lives here on earth, it matters to me what she would think of the choices I have made. She still challenges me to act in a way that would make her proud. What better legacy could one leave than to tweak the moral conscience of others and spur them on towards being persons of character?

MY EVERYDAY HERO
By Ryan Tool

I was an 18-year-old freshman at a small university in Minnesota when I first met Tom B., my favorite professor. It was the first time I had ever lived away from home and had spent most of my life preparing to go to college. I was filled with anticipation for the growth and development I would experience. I knew it was here that I would gain the skills to go forth into the world and be successful. Tom helped me to do this, but just as importantly, he helped me reevaluate my ideas of success.

As a freshman, I was required to take a course called Inquiry. We discussed books, debated current issues, and were taught how to become critical thinkers. We were not learning a particular subject area but rather learning to be better students. Most of my peers were not thrilled with the class, but I enjoyed it.

One day all the Inquiry classes had to meet in the big lecture hall. We were going to listen to a presentation from a guest speaker named Dr. B. The room darkened and Aerosmith's "Something's Wrong With the World Today" came blasting out. While the music played, a slide show portraying pollution, waste, hunger, homeless people, and our society's obsession with beauty and objects flashed across the screen. Then Tom came out and talked about two contrasting lifestyles: "The One with the Most Toys Wins" versus "All My Relations." The terms he used were new to me, but the ideas made sense. This message was relevant for me to ponder my goals in life — materialistic things versus enduring personal relationships. I was able to examine my life in a different light. Most importantly, I left the lecture hall that day with my curiosity piqued. I wanted to hear more of this man's wisdom and ideas about life.

I learned that Tom led a group called Passage that met weekly. I started to attend, and it became one of the best parts of my educational experience. Passage was set up to help students gain some understanding of themselves and their relationships, values, and lives. It was about initiation, moving from youth to adulthood. I received so much knowledge about the world around me and myself. I was able to clarify the importance of universal truths and enduring values. I believe that I would be lost now if I had not had the Passage experience.

Tom is a hero because he put so much energy into helping us to avoid some of the pain he had experienced in his own life. Or if we could not avoid the pain, then at least we would have some tools in order to deal with it. One thing he often told us was, "What you don't know can hurt you." As a younger man, Tom was a high-ranking executive. He was all about power and control. Compromise did not make sense to him; there was one right way to get things done. He was not in touch with those around him or himself. He soon found that he was way off balance. His marriage was no longer healthy, and he did not like his work. He felt lost and confused. After getting divorced and quitting his job, Tom was able to live with a Lakota Medicine Man. It was during this time that he dealt with the pain of his life and began to regain his balance.

If character is defined as "doing what is right even if it costs you more than you want to pay," then I believe without a doubt that Tom is a person of great character. Although Tom had knowledge and skills in other fields that could gain him more money and security, he chose to be a counselor. He wanted to use his experience to help others. He remained true to himself by doing something that made a difference in the lives of others.

I give a lot of credit to Tom for accepting a university position. It did not offer the highest pay or the greatest status, but it allowed him to do something he cared deeply about. He knew there was much pain and confusion in becoming an adult. He also knew that young people needed to be taught how to navigate this life transition effectively. Instead of just going along with the status quo and remaining safe, he chose to reach out to young people. None of his work, time, or energy with the Passage group was included in his job description.

As Passage progressed, Tom knew we needed a more private place for meditation, so he set aside a room in his small house just for us. Now he was sharing not only his time but also his home. Tom also sought out other adults to come and share with us, and he got each of us involved with a personal mentor.

Most importantly, Tom gave of himself. He shared with us his mistakes and embarrassments. He spent time planning and preparing for us. I even think he prayed for us. As a culmination of Passage, he set up an initiation ritual. In order to prepare for this, he fasted for a few days. A fast was his way of giving of himself. He was busy with his career and family, but he allowed us to consume so much of him because he knew we needed it. This is a hero.

One important thing Tom taught us was decision-making. Tom spends a good deal of his life preparing himself to make decisions. He sets aside time daily to meditate. As a result of this time, he has been able to re-discover values important to him and others. He defines values as "the things that pull you through life." They are the essence of what you stand for. Because he knows his values, he is able to make decisions. He compares his information with what he values. This is the starting point of an ethical decision-making process, but just a starting point.

Obviously we often have to decide between values that are in conflict. Tom taught us to do this by listening. He said most people are great at asking questions, but very few wait and listen for the answer. He put a lot of thought into his decisions, but he also tried to spend time just being.

In making ethical decisions, I believe Tom thought about the cost to himself last. He thought about his family, his friends, his community, and his relationship to the earth. He wanted the best for all of them. He also thought about his fears and worries, but whatever they were, he was not afraid to act even if it did put a larger burden on his shoulders. He knew he would have help.

I would love to live in a community of Tom B's. It would certainly be a much different community from the one I live in now. I think one large difference would be that people's top priority would be their relationships with themselves and others rather than on work and achieving status symbols. Therefore, people would work less. They would live in smaller houses with fewer gadgets. People would spend more time socializing with one other. They would be able to receive support from more people than just members of their immediate family. There would be no ill will towards anyone. I think there would be much less conflict and stress in personal interactions. People would find more depth in their souls. They would take more time to find meaning in their lives. They would have time to savor nature and develop a personal understanding of God. If the community were filled with Toms, economic development might slow, but spiritual development and self-esteem would blossom.

Tom was and still is a person of strong character and strong ethics. He demonstrated this every day in what he chose to do and how he interacted with others. I have a deep respect for the way he has defined his values and chosen to live his life. He has helped to put me on the path to becoming a fully-developed person. I now know that there is a lot more to being a man than being strong, powerful, and independent. I am very fortunate to have known this everyday hero.

MY EVERYDAY HERO
By Heather Kennedy

What makes an everyday hero? We have all seen heroes in movies, television sitcoms, and even a few on the six o'clock news. We each have our own concept of what a hero should be like, and if you ask a hundred people that seemingly simple question, you will probably receive a hundred different answers. To be a real hero is to display trust, respect, responsibility, fairness, caring, and good citizenship, and to live your life by these six pillars of character. I wish I could say that there are a hundred people in my life who have shown this excellence of character and who are everyday heroes, but the truth is there are very few. However, there is one individual who comes first to mind — an individual whose strong influence and impeccable character has touched my life in many ways, even though I have not spoken to her in years.

My everyday hero is Julie Poepple, one of the best teachers I ever had. Julie is a high school English and psychology teacher in a small town in South Dakota. The first time I was a student in Julie's class was my freshman year of high school. It was a time in my life when I needed guidance and a positive influence. Like many kids that age, I was searching for my identity and feeling insecure and unsure of myself. On the first day of class, Julie stood before us and explained the rules of her classroom. She outlined the grading system and her expectations for assignments just as several other teachers had; however, she also told us that if we needed help we could come to her and her door would always be open to us. She let us know that she would do her best to help us learn and that she took her classes very seriously. On that very first day I began to trust Julie because she had made a commitment to us. Trustworthiness is an important aspect of character because it involves honesty, integrity, and loyalty. Julie is trustworthy in all things, and she demands that same trustworthiness from both students and fellow faculty members. At times, she has had to stand up to students and confront them with breaking her trust by cheating or lying. She always gives the students the opportunity to redeem themselves by stepping forward and being honest. She teaches them that we all make mistakes, but one must own up to those mistakes, accept the consequences, and grow from them. Julie teaches these principles but is never self-righteous; she admits her mistakes freely, even when they could have remained hidden. She also uses them as an opportunity to teach others and to improve herself. In fact, Julie often told us that she would not expect us to learn anything that she herself did not model. These were words she lived by. I have never met anyone except Julie who truly lives by the principles that they teach.

Respect and tolerance for individual differences is a characteristic that is especially prevalent in Julie. In her psychology classes, Julie focused on both individuality and similarities among people. Her lectures stressed that individual differences give the world color and dimension. She warned that stereotyping and judging others would diminish our ability to see the world as it really is. We needed to base our conclusions about people and events on facts and first-hand experiences instead of preconceived ideas. At the same time, she demonstrated to her students that every person was our equal and had thoughts, feelings, and needs that were similar to our own. In one class activity, she wrote a general personality description for adolescents — but didn't tell us at first that it was general. The description included statements such as, "You feel that no one really understands you" and "Sometimes you feel lonely and unsure of yourself." She then wrote the name of every student on a separate copy of the paper and handed each of us our own copy. After instructing us to read the "personal" descriptions of ourselves, she asked how accurately we would rate her descriptions. Nearly all of the class said she was extremely accurate in her assessment of our feelings, fears, and characteristics. She then asked us to share our descriptions with the person behind us. At first, we were horrified that someone else would know these feelings and thoughts, but we did as we were instructed. As we read our partners' papers, we realized they were identical to our own and saw that we had a great deal in common regardless of our individuality; we all had the same basic needs and fears. At that moment, I realized that we were all equal. That lesson is still with me today. When I see someone at work or in the grocery store who seems very different from myself, I remember that they, too, have similar fears, needs, and thoughts common to all of us. Julie has worked with students from all different backgrounds and cultures in her profession and has treated each individual with respect and tolerance. Through her teaching and by her example, she has passed this respect on to her students.

The characteristic of responsibility demands that one better oneself and advance beyond one's current position or education. It also includes the obligation to contribute something to society. Julie has been in the teaching profession for many years; however, she is not stagnant. Everyday she learns something new through teaching others, through life experiences, and through the continuing education required to renew her teaching certificate. Through her work Julie is constantly making contributions to society. By being a strong role model and responsible citizen, Julie, like all teachers, helps to shape the minds and values of children everyday. Teachers are directly and indirectly responsible for educating students in academic as well as ethical, moral, and social realms. Teachers have the power to influence the future of our country through instruction and by example. By taking her commitment to education seriously, Julie has fulfilled this responsibility to the greatest of her potential.

Another quality of good character that Julie possesses and displays is that of fairness. She is consistent and fair in her assignments and her grading. Julie has very high standards for her students; she expects them to meet the strict criteria that she

defines clearly at the beginning of each assignment. I remember
one incident that occurred in Julie's psychology class when I
was a junior. Julie gave a particularly difficult test over several
chapters, and the average score on the exam was quite low. The
day she handed the tests back she asked us if we thought the test
was fair. Of course we all said no, and she proceeded to ask us
questions about the chapters we had studied. We went over each
question on the test and discussed the right and wrong answers
for the entire period. At the end of the class she announced
that she would give a second test the following day because she
believed that her test had missed the mark. For her to concede
that the test had been an invalid measure of our knowledge,
made us realize that she was not out to fail us; she really cared
whether or not we were learning from her. She truly wanted to
be fair.

Julie takes an active interest in the well-being of all of her
students. She is one of the most caring teachers I have ever
met. Caring refers to bringing out the best in people. It means
being sympathetic to others' feelings and needs. Throughout
my high school years, Julie and I had contact through classes
and yearbook committee. She knew some of the difficult things
I was going through, and she was always that little voice telling
me that I was okay. She made me feel capable and strong in
subtle ways. To this day, I don't honestly know if these messages
were intentional or if it was just Julie being Julie.

When I graduated from high school, Julie gave me a picture
frame with a verse she had written. It said, "If I could give you
but one gift it would be the ability to see yourself as others truly
see you." I still have that verse. I read it quite often, and it has
had a great impact on my life. Every time I start to feel that I
cannot succeed or accomplish something in my life, I read the
verse and realize that I can and that I have already accomplished
so much. Knowing that she believed in my ability even when I
did not, made me believe in it, too. That is her way of bringing

out the best in people. To have someone you hold in such high regard believe in *you* is an amazing and compelling thing.

The final component of character is citizenship. Julie is a very selfless and giving woman. She always goes above and beyond what is asked of her. She understands that we are all connected and that by helping someone else we make a positive difference in the lives of many. Julie does not ask for external rewards, and she does not always receive a "thank-you" for what she does, but she still continues to behave as a person of great character.

She maintains a positive outlook on life and refuses to dwell on negativity. One example of this can be found in her experiences with her son. Julie's first son, Adam, is developmentally disabled; however, from the very beginning of his physical therapy, Julie never concentrated on his limitations. Instead, she would come to class thankful for each little bit of progress he made. She has that attitude about all things; she is always looking for the positive. When others cannot see past their problems, she reminds them that they still have much to be thankful for and that it is the little everyday things that make life meaningful.

Julie is my everyday hero. She lives her life with integrity, respect, responsibility, fairness, caring, and citizenship. She has made a difference in the lives of each of her students and countless others who know her. People like Julie are rare in the world today, and they seldom receive the applause and gratitude they deserve. We don't hear their names spoken on the news or see their pictures on the front page of the newspaper, and sadly, we don't often think to say "thank-you." More of us need to look at the people we interact with everyday who positively affect our lives and give them the credit and thanks that they deserve. I have waited too long to thank Julie for enriching my life. I will not wait any longer to tell her how much I appreciated her encouraging spirit!

IV. THE EVERYDAY HEROES OF HIGH SCHOOL STUDENTS

MY EVERYDAY HERO
By Mellissa Adams

My everyday hero is my mom. She is not only my mother but one of my best friends, too. My everyday hero is not a wonder woman with magical powers that make all my problems go away. No. My everyday hero is a petite, brown-haired, honey-brown-eyed woman with split ends. She goes to work every day (except for Wednesday), works a part-time job, and then comes home to clean house, pick me up from school, cook dinner, do the dishes — and then she barely has time to sit down for her afternoon nap. Praise God for moms! She puts half her paycheck towards my school education, just because she wanted me to go to a Christian school.

My everyday hero helps me with my everyday problems. My everyday problems consist of homework, friends, boyfriends, teachers, math, science, things I hear people say about me, the way my locker is totally trashed, and questions about the why, what, how come, and what for. If I have a question about life, marriage, family, friends, or the birds and the bees, my mom will tell me. Why? Because my mom wants to keep me informed about the world.

Mom is my teacher. She's taught me why not to get pregnant before I get married. She's shown me to be ready for love, but not to act on it yet. She tells me about loving a man and being a good mother at the same time. Mom has taught me to cook stir-fry, lasagna, chicken noodle soup, and all my favorite dinners and desserts. Mom teaches me about God, how to have devotions every day, how to pray for a future husband and career. Mom teaches me about being a housewife — not just by telling me things, but by working while I'm busy explaining to her the latest crisis and catastrophe in my life. While I talk, she keeps doing her dishes and tells me how to go about solving my problems. I ask her advice on everything. Not only does she give me advice;

she gives me *good* advice. There's a difference. My mom tells me how to be a better person without changing myself completely.

My mom chooses to be a mother to me. It's not like she's just obligated to be my mom; she chooses to be my mom and put up with me. She chooses to put up with a sixteen-year-old who would rather be a house cat than go outside and do something. A sixteen-year-old who would rather watch a movie that she's seen a million times over than go to a movie that has just come out. I ask my mom if I bore her with my trivial little problems in life and she just laughs, shakes her head, and says, "No, honey, I don't mind, tell me everything."

Mom has helped me in so many ways that I wouldn't be able to name them all, except the ones that really stick out in my mind. Like the time I broke up with the guy I thought I was going to marry. When I came into the living room, fists clenched and tears threatening to pour over, she told me one thing: "Okay, be mad and angry now, but then forgive and be done with it." She also told me that time heals all wounds, but I didn't believe her...then. I found out my life really does go on whether or not that ex-boyfriend wakes up to automatically think of me. Mom helped me to get over myself. I am so self-conscious when it comes to my body. She told me that I won't really get used to my body until I'm around twenty. She tells me I'm a beautiful girl and she wishes that she had my eyes (because my eyes are hazel-gray) when she was in school. She lifts me up in the best way, and also scorns me when I over-exaggerate. She's my mom.

And when I finally have children, and if Mom is gone to heaven, I'll tell my kids about a wonderful woman who wasn't perfect but was pretty close. She had her faults like the rest of us, but she did other things to make up for them. I will tell them of the times when I would pick up the phone and everyone would think that I was Mom, or when I walked into my class and a friend thought I looked exactly like my mother. "Mirror, mirror, on the wall, I'm like my mother after all." I pray I'm like my mom, because she's my everyday hero.

MY EVERYDAY HEROES

By Bethany Carr

John and Rachael Debruin are the youth leaders at our church. John leads "The Way" youth group. Rachel teaches the girl's Bible study. They also organize youth group activities at times. Both are actively involved in the church.

John and Rachael Debruin really care about us and it shows. Whenever one of us needs someone to talk to, they're always available. They are always willing to pray for us and are very encouraging. We can always trust them, and we can always count on them to give us moral support. It's their support, encouragement, and prayers that help me get through hard times.

One reason I've always looked up to John and Rachael is because they take the time to talk to us and pray for us. Last year, for instance, when we were in Mexico on a mission trip, my dad unexpectedly ended up in the hospital. They prayed for our family and were very encouraging to Dad and me. They were also there for us, to support us. I am grateful for all they did. It was a *huge* help.

Another time last year, when I was going through a *really* tough time, Rachael and John spent time talking to me. They didn't just sit down for a minute and say a few words, either. They really listened and showed an interest in what I was saying. After I had finished, they encouraged me to trust God and keep going. Also, they promised to pray for me. What they did then will never be forgotten. They were always there for me when I needed their support. It meant a lot to me.

Another reason I look up to John and Rachael is because they have a strong faith in God and consistently walk with him. One can really see God working in their lives and using them in his ministry. Also, they're honest about their walk with God. Neither one ever pretends to be "perfect." They each admit to us that they make mistakes just like everybody else. If John or Rachael are struggling with something, they don't put on an act. They're honest. Their honesty and faith are a strong encouragement.

Rachael and John's faith in God was put to the test when our youth group began supporting a trip to Hungary. John felt God was calling him to go on the trip. The weeks during which he would be gone would be close to their baby's due date. It was certainly going to be a risk! They were willing, however, to trust God and leave the problems for Him to solve.

John and Rachael's encouragement and support will always be remembered. They willingly give of their time to people who need prayer, advice, or just someone to talk to. Their honesty and strong faith have been a source of encouragement. Also, they have set a good example for the kids in our youth group. I am extremely grateful to God for allowing me to have them as examples to follow and as people to look up to.

Soon, they will be having a boy or a girl. Rachael and John, from what I've seen so far, are going to make *great* parents. I can only hope that someday, I can set a good example for younger believers as they have done for us.

MY EVERYDAY HEROES
By Ashley Enright

To write about one hero is kind of hard because I have so many people I look up to and admire. I can narrow it down to two people, though. One hero is my Aunt Diane. My other hero is my cousin Kara, my Aunt Diane's daughter. These two people are very special to me, and hopefully someday I will grow up to be just like them!

One of my main reasons for admiring my Aunt Diane is because of her personality. She is a very funny person to be around. She's also very fun to be around. When I go over to her house just to hang out, she is always asking me how I am doing and if I need to talk to anyone about any problems. Aunt Diane is a very caring person. She really cares about her nieces and nephews a lot. She does whatever she can to help them out when they are in some kind of trouble, whether it's giving them advice on what to do or defending them when she knows that they didn't do anything wrong. It's also obvious that she loves her husband and her children very much. Her main goal in life is to make sure that her family is taken care of. I think that is just an encouragement to me for when I am older and have a family of my own. Don't you think that would be an encouragement to you too?

If my Aunt Diane ever reads this, I would just want to thank her for being a good aunt to me and for always being there when I needed someone to talk to.

My other hero, Kara, is just like her mom in many ways. She is a very humorous person. Everything that she says is always funny, even when she isn't trying to be funny. Kara also really cares about herself. That may sound really selfish, as if all she cares about is herself, but that is not what I mean at all. She is a very smart person and very disciplined about her studies in school. When she was in high school, she disciplined herself not to get distracted from her studies. For example, if one of her friends called her, she would not talk to them until she was done with all her homework or whatever she was doing at the time. Most people would just ignore their studies and talk to their friends. It is common to do that. How many people do you know who like doing schoolwork? I know for myself that I hate doing my schoolwork just because I'm a very lazy person, and I am paying for it, too! I know for Kara, though, that it has all paid off. She now is in a very good school in Washington and is majoring in journalism. In addition to doing so well in college, she has been accepted to a very good school in Europe. I am very proud of the success she has experienced.

Another way that I know she cares about herself is her commitment to self-improvement. Kara used to smoke a lot until one day she realized how much she was destroying her body and how unhealthy it made her look. She decided to quit and start going to the gym to work out. Kara also decided to take me along with her when she went to work out. Let me tell you, she is a very strong and a very determined person. For example, they had these stairs that kept going up and down, and you had to stay on them. It was kind of like walking up and down your stairs at home but a smaller version of them. She walked on them for 20 minutes! Talk about hard work. It must have been hard to do but she knew it was good for her. Also, every year there is a run-a-thon for children with diseases; the runners have to run for about six miles, I think, and she does this every year without stopping! I know these reasons aren't the best examples, but they are the reasons why I look up to her so much. Just little things about her.

If Kara is able to read this, I really want to thank her for showing me how to be more disciplined and for being a good example to me!

Kara and Diane have much in common. They are both excellent role models for me and have had a tremendous impact on my life in a positive way. Thank you both!

MY EVERYDAY HEROES
By Ashleigh Hester

A hero is someone you look up to and have respect for. They seem to always know all the right things to say. You might not even know them very well, but they have done good for someone or done a deed that you really respected. I have had many people come in and out of my life, and some have made an impression on me that will remain forever in my heart.

In my life, I have many heroes. Two of them are my parents. No matter what I do or how I act, they are always there to help me back up again. I may sometimes show them that I don't care, or that I don't really need them, but really if I didn't have them I wouldn't be the way I am now. Occasionally, I will get mad or yell at them and say rude things to hurt their feelings. They still never give up on me. Often they think they have failed or done something wrong. They haven't. They have always been here for me and always will. My mom stays home just so she can clean the house and make everything nice for us. Now that is someone worth looking up to!

Another person who has really had an impact on my life is Brandy Stewart. Brandy is one of my very good friends even though she is 20 and a lot older than I am. She is such a nice person; it seems like she never has anything mean or hurtful to say. Everything that she says and does is to build people up and not tear them down. This means a lot to me because I often have a hard time saying nice things to people. When she is around, I feel like it is so much better to be nice. She has been such an encouragement to me and I will always be grateful for what she has done. Brandy is also very truthful. I don't think she would ever lie to me. Trust is something that you have to have in a friend. You can't have a hero that you don't trust or don't think does the right thing.

As you can see, a hero is not just anyone. It is someone you look up to, respect, and a good friend who is always there for you. Someone else who is my hero is my Uncle Ralph. When my uncle was younger, he wasn't a very good Christian. He did a lot of really bad things that he will always be able to look back and remember. I have always loved and respected my uncle but not as much as I do now. Lately I have really seen a change in him that amazes me. A while ago, my uncle started to show a deeper commitment to going to church more. We all could see a difference in his spiritual and physical outlook. Now he is always doing something. He has been taking care of his kids while my Aunt Sharon is in the hospital. Ever since she has gone to the hospital, he has had to go to work and find places for the kids to go. He visits his wife and makes time to spend with his kids. I think that would be so hard to do. He barely has any time to rest or anything, and he is still at church every Sunday. I really look up to him for doing this. It shows me how I want to be someday when I have a family of my own.

One last person who I really look up to is a lady from my church named Miss Lee. She really astounds me. She has been through so much pain. Her husband left her a few years ago, leaving her with her three kids. Now she only has two of the three because one went to live with his dad. Through it all, I know it is only by God's grace that she can be so happy and cheerful all the time. She has such a good heart. She never wants anything for herself. She is always giving, no matter what. I sometimes don't understand how people who go through such hard times in their lives can still look ahead and see God. I can see God through her life and it has helped me to see how I need to have a happy and giving heart too, no matter what happens in my life. Sometimes I might think that my life is bad, but then I see someone else who has many more problems than I have. They are still happy and it really encourages me to do the same.

Though these are people who I should look up to and who are very good, they aren't perfect. God is the only one who is perfect. He is my hero and He should be everyone's hero. What He did no one else could ever do. He gave His life so that we could be saved and live forever with Him. Sometimes we forget that He should be our hero. A lot of people worship many things and God is not one of them. They are really missing out on something special. God loves us more than anyone and always will. We can never lose his love, no matter what we do. People always make mistakes and people will come into your life and will hurt you sometimes, but you don't need to worry because God will always be right with you until the end.

Through all these people, God has shown many different things that have helped in my life. I can see now that a hero is more than someone on TV who you like. It is someone who truly cares about people, and it shows through his or her life.

MY EVERYDAY HERO
by Cassandra Keltz

I am a 14-year-old teen, and I am lucky to have such a great person as my hero: my mom, Joanne Brokaw. Although Jesus Christ is my all-time hero, my mom has definitely proven herself to be a hero. My mom has shown me strength, love and encouragement throughout my life, and what a legacy she will leave behind. Although many people don't think of their mothers as heroes, I definitely do.

My mom was an unmarried woman when she was pregnant with me. She was in a relationship with a man whom she was willing to marry, but he wouldn't get married. My biological father wanted my mom to have an abortion, but she refused. He also wanted her to give me up for adoption after I was born. However, again she refused. I am so thankful for my mom's decision. The Lord has now blessed me with a great family and a step-father. Through that experience, my mom showed so much strength. My mom had a problem that would change her life, but instead of feeling sorry for herself, she made it through. That took so much courage, I'm sure. My mom has also helped me with my normal growing-up stuff. When I have a problem, the first person I turn to is my mom. (She does come after the Lord, however.)

My mom has a way of helping me with situations that I don't think I can get through on my own. She is my best friend on earth. I truly thank the Lord for her willingness to help me even with stupid stuff about guys. I know my mom has been where I am now, and she can always relate to what I am going through.

My mom helps me, but she also helps my friends. I transferred schools this year to an awesome Christian school. In my old school, however, there were so many problems. My friends were pretty much all having a hard time with their lives. I know that my friends were having such a hard time because they were without the one person who could heal them from such pain, Jesus Christ. I always told my friends that, but my mom has a way of "showing" to them that they need Jesus. My mom is always there, though, to be the responsible adult. She has a way of connecting with my friends, teenagers in general, that is very cool.

I remember when one of my friends came over and was just sitting on my living room floor crying her eyes out because she couldn't take her life anymore. She was just so upset. Being her friend, I tried as hard as I could to comfort her, but I could only do so much. I am not a very comforting person. That was just not the spiritual gift that the Lord bestowed on me. My mom was there, however, and she knew just what to do. Not only did that prove what a good mother she was, but also how she can be a friend. My mom and the Holy Spirit working as a team were able to help my friend to the point where she was willing to turn to her family (they were her problem in the first place). It wasn't long after that experience that my friends were calling my mom on the phone, instead of me. That was an experience itself! I was happy that my friends all had an adult to look up to. It is such a comforting thing when you know someone older than you is there.

My mom helps adults, too. A few years back, my mom opened up her own business, a tea shop. She loves tea very much. She knew a lot of factual information about tea. Some people would come to the store and talk about tea for hours with her. It was pretty boring to me, because at 14 years I don't really care about the factual information of tea. Anyway, my mom went through a lot of financial difficulties, and the Lord was going through it with us. Even through that time, however, my mom was an encouragement to the Lord. When a customer walked into the store and began to talk with my mom, she was constantly speaking of the Lord. I know that people could see God's light through her; I remember people coming to the store and just talking about the Lord with her, because they knew she was a Christian. My mom and I met some very cool people and it was fun, but eventually her little business shut down. She closed the store and began working out of the house. Eventually she stopped. My point is that my mom took every opportunity to serve the Lord, and she did it well. If my mom worked at McDonalds I believe that she would still serve the Lord the same as if she had money like Bill Gates. She leaves an impact on people; it's very cool.

I think the best thing about my mom is that she can always make me laugh. This lady is so funny! She just makes up all these impressions of animals. I know that sounds weird—but it always makes me laugh. And she makes my friends laugh, too. It's cool when I'm not the only person laughing at my mom's antics.

My mom proved her strength again to me when she suffered from cancer in June of 1999. It was a pretty scary thing for me; I can't imagine how it was for her. My mom went through a lot of emotional problems during that time, and it was interesting having her need me, like I always needed her. I prayed for her so much, and the Lord was awesome as always and He healed her completely. During this time of struggle, however, my mom never lost her. That funny side of her, or that caring side of her. Another thing about her cancer experience that was truly amazing is that she didn't fall from the Lord. Instead she grew closer to him. She carried Bible verses around with her and memorized verses that were comforting to her. She had never done that before, as far as I know. Not only did that help her, but it was an encouragement to me. I used to struggle a lot with keeping that fire for the Lord. Little trials that the Lord put me through usually caused me to drift away. My mom didn't hit a little stubblestone with this cancer, though; she hit a brick wall. And throughout that time she was always faithful to the Lord God! It was so amazing. That experience was so difficult for all of my family, but now it's all right. She is healed. My mom was so faithful to the Lord that He decided she had suffered enough and let her have peace with cancer. It was so amazing how God worked in our lives. And it's so good to have a mom who is in love with the Lord as much as she is. It keeps me "on my toes."

All in all, I just love my mom. She is my hero, my best friend, and a servant to Jesus Christ. She strives for the best and adds light to the lives of people. It is a true blessing to have her for a mother, and I thank the Lord for her. I honestly can say I don't know what I would do without her. She is my everyday hero, and I love her very much.

MY EVERYDAY HERO
By Nicole Grossglass

Do you know anyone who is one hundred percent honest, always caring, responsible, fair, thoroughly respectful, and respected? I do. My grandmother, Eleanor Grossglass, is my everyday hero. At the age of four or five I started to call her Lellie. My family was always at her place, and we were so close that I started to call her "Mom." When she realized the mistake and that I wouldn't call her Grandma, she and my mom tried to get me to call her "Ellie" (short for Eleanor). All of a sudden I came up with Lellie, and she loved it.

Lellie is a small, petite lady who is half Italian. She has very dark skin and I've always admired the graceful air with which she does things. Just last week I was admiring how she seems to glide and do everything with a slow, gradual motion — so graceful with her careful, cautious disposition. I even like to watch her make grocery lists because she writes with such care and neatness, and I like to see her clean because she takes her time and seems to have great concern with the job at hand.

My sisters and I are her only grandchildren, and I admit I don't mind it when they spoil us. But my grandparents do it in such a humble, quiet way that unless you talked to us about it, you wouldn't know. She takes us on her own at Christmas and Easter to go shopping for dresses for those occasions. One example of her honesty is when we try on dresses. This past week, I went to the mall and I was trying on dresses. She asked to see them and I showed each and every one to her. As I tried on different dresses, she was completely honest in a way that made me feel comfortable and that wouldn't hurt anyone's feelings.

Whenever one of my sisters and I get into an argument, she listens to both our sides and decides fairly without a hint of favoritism. I have always loved her gentle spirit, too. She explains things in a way that makes sense, and the way she speaks makes it sound as if she practices the words she's choosing. Whenever I make a mistake, she doesn't condemn or yell at me; she rather corrects me and shows me in a quiet way how to do things differently.

Another thing I admire about Lellie is that she doesn't gossip or lie. Now, gossiping and lying are some of the hardest things to avoid, and when I tell her about things that are going on, she's careful about how she responds. My grandfather and grandmother deal with a lot of people, and I've never seen her criticize or put anyone down before giving them the benefit of the doubt. Sometimes I think she is too nice and kind, but that is my favorite thing about her. I feel I can be anyone around her, and that makes me feel good.

I also love to watch her give advice. She doesn't do it in a way that would reveal the person's weakness; instead, she is almost apologetic about being the one to say something. I admire her relationship with the Lord, too. Her relationship is very solid and strong, and she never pushes her faith on people or brags about the stability of her faith.

I have learned some things about Lellie from my dad and mom and Lellie herself that make me admire her even more. After my dad was born, she and my grandfather had a baby girl. Their daughter lived only one and a half days before dying of a brain problem. Sometimes if we mention her name at her birthday or a holiday, Lellie gets teary-eyed and I know she is whispering for God's help to stay strong. She has faced other difficulties, too. Her childhood wasn't easy, and her family were not all Christians, but she has turned out to be the best grandmother in the world, someone who is willing to sacrifice for others. This past year my grandfather was "promoted" from being the senior pastor of our church to the secretary treasurer of the New York State district. They had to move from being right around the corner from us to an hour and a half away. They are never home and are always traveling to speak at a church here or to do a favor for a church there. Lellie sometimes looks exhausted when we see her, but her love for my grandpa and for the Lord and His plan for their lives keeps the twinkle in her eye —especially whenever she ends up taking care of my three little sisters and me! Sometimes just seeing her makes me want to do things for her. Her smile and her compassionate way of serving others makes me want to pick up a dishrag and wash the dishes or clear off the dinner table or give her a break by answering the telephone.

One example of her love for me occurred when I was seven or eight. My grandmother is very elegant; she and my grandfather are very well off, and as a child I grew accustomed to her crystal and jewels, along with the glass and marble statues and other lovely things she had around the house. She never showed off; these things just suited her, and she enjoyed picking out things that sparkled and that were original. Well, in one of their old houses, she had her crystal collection dispersed across the entertainment center. On a lower shelf, unfortunately within my reach, she had a crystal bowl that had a lot of small, rounded jewels and gems. They began to fascinate me, and I was determined to be like Lellie and keep something sparkling in my room, too. So, when no one was looking, I would take one or two of the eye-catching stones. I knew it was wrong and I felt badly, but even at that young age I admired my grandmother and wanted to be just like her. Because I knew what I was doing was wrong and because I knew the stones were expensive, I thought that if I left the house with one something would give me away — maybe a buzzer or alarm. I therefore decided to play it safe for awhile and hide them in a cabinet in the room I always stayed in. Since we lived nearby and were at Lellie's a lot, the bowl's quantity of stones was soon dwindling. The fact that this decrease in quantity was very obvious escaped my seven-year-old mind; I thought my parents and grandparents wouldn't possibly notice. Another thing that escaped me was that women keep their houses clean and like to go over the entire house every few weeks.

A few weeks went by and I realized Lellie knew. I was confused because she didn't say anything; I no longer took as many stones as before, and took them less often. One weekend we left Lellie's, and the next time we returned, the bowl seemed to be filled. Later I discovered my drawer was empty. Much to my relief, nothing was said at dinner, but Lellie talked to my parents about something before we left. The next day on the way back to Lellie's, my parents expressed their anger and disappointment. By the time we got to Lellie's house, I was quite afraid of her reaction. When my parents left, my grandmother took me to my room and sat me on the bed.

"Nicole," she said quietly, and at the sound of her soft, sad voice, I began to cry. "I was very disappointed in you when I realized you were taking my crystal stones from their bowl."

"I'm so sorry, Lellie," I whimpered. "I didn't mean to hurt you. I'm so sorry. Are you mad at me?"

"No, I wasn't mad at you," Lellie explained gently as she pulled me into her lap and hugged me. "I was just very disappointed."

From then on I vowed to do things the way Lellie did and vowed that I would never disappoint her again. I remember thinking that I would rather she had been angry and spanked me than hug me and look at me with those sad, disappointed eyes. To this day, if I do something wrong, I feel so badly when I'm scolded by Lellie or my grandfather. I learned my lesson, and I loved Lellie all the more for teaching it to me.

I know for sure that she loves me and no matter how rough it gets, she always says, "I'm here, you know that, I'm here." It's hard when she says that now because I don't see her a lot, but she knows I like to hear it because even when we are making ice cream sundaes and watching a movie, she might lean over and whisper in her gentle, calming voice those words: "I'm here, you know that, I'm here." I've never doubted her or my grandfather's love, and when I lose them I know it'll be really hard. Until then, though, I'd like to cherish today and hope for another tomorrow with my everyday hero, my Lellie.

V. THE LEGACIES OF EVERYDAY HEROES

"It is true I am only one. But I am one. And the fact that I cannot do everything will not stop me from doing what I can do."
— Edward Hale

The everyday heroes described in these stories have left wonderful legacies that will last forever. Their altruistic spirits have touched many as a result of their commitment to seize the opportunity to do the right thing on a consistent basis. These individuals of great character all use the six pillars as their guiding principles, regardless of life's challenges.

The eternal legacies result from being motivated to help others overcome adversity. Regardless of the challenge — grief issues, eating disorders, cancer, abuse, disabilities, poverty — people of character see those challenges as opportunities to demonstrate their caring and responsible spirits. You can trust an everyday hero not to dismiss concerns as a burden but rather view adversity as a chance to make a positive difference. They instill a sense of hope, affirmation, and encouragement. As a result, the recipients of their generous acts are filled with a newly-found courage. Scott Peck, famous psychiatrist and author, stated, "courage is the capacity to go ahead in spite of the fear, or in spite of the pain."

Everyday heroes appear to develop a mission in life that includes looking for ways to bring out the best in others. They take personal responsibility for living lives of character by treating themselves and others with love, care, and respect while remaining mindful of a broader purpose of becoming trustworthy, fair, and good citizens. Their purpose in life is fueled by a zest for living and a commitment to go after life proactively. As President John F. Kennedy stated, "There are costs and risks to a program of action, but they are far less than the long range risks and costs of comfortable inaction." Thriving in life results from being intentional about taking control and making useful, life-enriching choices that flow from a clear purpose in life. The by-product of their exuberance for living is the positive energy that radiates to others in the form of encouragement.

Imagine a world composed of individuals who possess great character. What would it be like if everyone were fully worthy of trust? Surely communication would be much more honest and authentic. The result of this would be vastly improved relationships. Individuals would feel much better sharing their thoughts and feelings openly, while the listener would not have the onerous task of trying to figure out what was *really* meant. Trust would be enhanced by kept promises as well. There would be little doubt regarding commitment, follow-up, arrival and departure times, and faithfulness. Loyalty would become the norm, and interpersonal conflicts would be confronted proactively, leading to solutions and an action-plan. Integrity would be pervasive as thoughts, words, and deeds would be in concert with each other. The positive impact on every relationship — with friends, marriage partners, colleagues, neighbors, communities, and the world — would be extraordinary.

What would the world look like if everyone were totally respectful? Every person would be treated as a social equal regardless of physical, racial, cultural, gender, or age differences. Differences of opinion would be welcomed even if they led to disagreements. Condescending remarks would disappear, and active listening would be the basis of every conversation. Creativity would be stimulated, and wonderful ideas would occur, leading to harmony and peaceful conditions in all social relationships. Good manners would be pervasive and there would be no sign of prejudice, harassment, manipulation, or coercion.

What would the world look like if everyone were totally responsible? Every individual would try as hard as possible in each of their most important life roles — as parents, spouses, significant others, friends, workers, community members, and volunteers. People would be responsible for managing their time in harmony with their priorities, including their spiritual, emotional, and physical well-being. Useful choices would be the norm while laziness, indifference, and poor choices would be reduced significantly. The world would reap the rewards of high yet efficient productivity with everyone flourishing by using their gifts for the benefit of society.

What would the world look like if everyone were totally fair? Equal opportunities would exist for every individual based on agreed-upon criteria for objective decision-making. Oppression would disappear with an increasing effort made towards open trade and achieving equal access to food, shelter, and technology. Evaluations would be made on relevant criteria, both in school, higher education, and at the work-site. Increased cooperation, interdependence, and charitable giving would help every country in the world to have access to education and optimal employment conditions. Consequences for useless behavior would be consistent and appropriate, thus decreasing irresponsible behavior.

What would the world look like if everyone were caring? People would seek out ways they could make a positive difference in the lives of others. Uncaring and hurtful remarks would not be spoken. There would be an outpouring of loving gestures, including displays of empathy and compassion. Positive statements and encouragement would be offered while people were alive rather than being reserved for funerals. There would be an absence of abuse, neglect, loneliness, and selfish behavior. Caring would also be extended to self-care, leading to wellness lifestyles and fulfilling careers.

What would the world be like if everyone were a good citizen? Politicians would be voted into office on appropriate criteria. Taxes would be fairly assessed, and laws would be established that are in the best interest of everyone. Our schools would all be equally impressive, connecting students with the best teachers available. The curriculums would be well-researched, and every student would have computers and internet access, giving them equal opportunities for learning. Every road, regardless of its location, would be safe in all types of weather conditions. Parks would be clean and would invite citizens to get away and enjoy the beauty of creation. Litter and graffiti would be nonexistent. Volunteerism and stewardship would increase significantly, improving living conditions for all people.

It is easy to believe that this description is idealistic and will never come to be. Fortunately, everyday heroes do not adopt this mentality, which is so often an excuse for inactivity. Although they will never be perfect, everyday heroes continue to try to make the world a better place. Cynicism only exacerbates the problems we have. Everyday heroes simply "roll-up their sleeves" and do the hard work of making the world a better place.

How does one become a person of character? Most individuals dedicated to living ethical lives attribute their moral lifestyles to respected individuals who taught them how to live, inspired them to be good people, and modeled principled behavior. The moral lessons they received were clear, consistent, and numerous. Encouragement accompanied useful choices and discipline followed poor decisions. Their role models did not expect perfection or obedience but rather advocated a life centered around the values of trustworthiness, respect, responsibility, caring, fairness, and good citizenship.

I have had remarkable role models in my own life. I could and probably should write a book about my parents, whose positive attitudes, endless giving, common sense, and incredible work ethic easily make them everyday heroes. My wife, who wakes up each day and looks at her calendar to see whose birthday or anniversary it is so she can write them a card, would also qualify. She demonstrates incredible caring and responsible behavior each and every day. Her volunteerism is a true gift to our community.

I can also think of relatives, friends, colleagues, coaches, and a few outstanding teachers who were devoted to bringing out the best in me. I hope they realize that their spirit provided the inspiration to write this book.

Will the world be better off as a result of your existence? Are you willing to consistently do the right thing even in the face of temptation and adversity? What kind of legacy will you leave? These are difficult questions to consider because our daily lives have become increasingly cluttered with endless "to do" lists. Too many people heed the message that they should get ahead at all costs. Unrestrained competitiveness is often the nemesis of principled living, promoting the illusion of meaningful living via the accumulation of wealth and material things. This selfish mindset encourages people to view others as roadblocks and contributes to a life of one-upmanship. As Michael Josephson stated, "When you decide to fight fire with fire all you get is the ashes of your own integrity." Additional enemies of integrity include, but are not limited to, fear, lack of will, impulsiveness, rationalization, procrastination, fatalism, cynicism, victim-ism, or "it's not my job-ism." As Edmund Burke stated, "All that is necessary for evil to triumph is for good people to do nothing."

Stephen Covey, well-known business consultant and author, believes that part of the problem is that "the world's value system is primarily focused on secondary greatness. It rewards and makes heroes out of incredibly strong and agile athletes, talented musicians and artists, gifted and persuasive speakers, powerful and wealthy business executives. But even though success may require the talents and skills that make up secondary greatness, long-term sustainable results and impact always come from primary greatness first — from tapping into the natural laws or principles that produce those results." The six pillars of character are the laws that produce primary greatness and our everyday heroes.

Anyone can achieve primary greatness by consistently making a positive difference in the lives of others. A desire to do what is right is what prompts the six pillars into action. Individuals of character look for ways to make a significant impact in the lives of others. Although they engage in moral acts because it's the right thing to do, they discover that life's positive energy is person to person. Their daily heroic acts are performed out of feelings of accomplishment, purposeful living, and fullness of life.

Does becoming an Everyday Hero seem overwhelming to you? It is easy to overestimate the cost of doing the right thing and underestimate the cost of failing to do so. Keep in mind that you do not have to be perfect, gifted, rich, great-looking, or have high self-esteem to be a person of character. The only question you have to answer is, "Am I willing to live by the six pillars of character and do the right thing, even if it costs me more than I want to pay on a consistent basis?" When you make a mistake, a commitment is made to make a more useful choice tomorrow.

Our world needs you to be a person of great character. As E.D. Hirsch stated, "We need to combat the widespread loss of heroes and moral ideals in the hearts and minds of young people. They need a meaningful frame of reference and awareness of individuals who bring the moral journey to life for them — individuals whose lives teach vital and memorable lessons." There is an urgent need for ethical individuals who are willing to be wonderful parents, relatives, volunteers, mentors, educators, colleagues, and friends. In the book *The Case for Character Education*, B. David Brooks and Frank G. Goble stated, "If we, as parents, educators, and community members don't solve this character deficit problem, we are doomed to live with the consequences. If we think that teen pregnancy, gangs, drug and alcohol abuse, school failure, a loss of civility, the lack of work ethic, and violence are the problem, then we are doomed to live with these symptoms. The problem is the lack of a moral compass, failure to instill values and expecting someone else to solve the problem." Everyday heroes do their part to address the core of the problem, slightly closing the hole in the moral ozone.

Our youth compose 27% of society and 100% of the future. In their book *Building Character in Schools*, Kevin Ryan and

Karen Bohlin assert that there are four primary reasons why young people engage in promiscuity, violence, or drug and alcohol abuse. They conclude that youngsters have a desire to belong; they are too often bored; they lack compelling interests or responsibilities to divert them from useless behaviors; and finally, they can easily find an escape from pain or meaninglessness in their lives. Ryan and Bohlin insist that all young people need an attentive ear, inspiration, love, structure, and friendship.

Stephen Covey agrees by stating that children need help to develop a sense of intrinsic worth and a vision for making unique, meaningful contributions to the world. The optimal process for encouraging growth is to teach by example. Always affirm and believe in them, avoid comparisons with others, promote involvement in school and extracurricular activities, and advocate the supreme importance of taking responsibility for their choices and resulting consequences. Adults can encourage youngsters to live with integrity as they reach toward their dreams and aspirations.

It seems clear that each youngster needs time, attention, and affection from good role models to thrive in a constantly changing society. Strong relationships between adults and young people appear to be the key to facilitating the moral maturity and development of our youth. Each day is an opportunity for young people to build stronger character by being exposed to positive role models that demonstrate how to be trustworthy, respectful, responsible, fair, caring, and a good citizen. Opportunities for teachable moments can be seized daily at home, school, youth organizations, church, and at work. The six pillars can become the benchmark for expected behaviors of adults and children. Promoting character can be accomplished by helping individuals become conscious of the six pillars, inspire commitment to internalize these values, and most importantly to become competent at decision-making. Moral maturity requires knowledge, reflection, judgment, and personal choice.

One of my responsibilities as a parent is to ensure that my children's basic needs are met, including the need to be loved and to love; to be whole and well; and to be free to live out their purpose in life. Furthermore, since they come into the world with a blank moral slate, I need to, as Plato stated, "bring their reason, spirit, and appetite into intelligent harmony." It will be difficult for me to teach values if I do not live by them. I must be careful not to sacrifice family time for work. It is true that nobody says on their deathbed, "I wish I would have spent more time at work." Let's face it: work doesn't love you back! Regrets in life are almost always relational in nature. Raising children of great character is very time-consuming, sometimes challenging, and always rewarding. It requires consistent teaching and discipline combined with a continual demonstration of the six pillars in action. My responsibility is made easier when I can partner with other caring adults including relatives, friends, teachers, school counselors, and clergy. Hopefully, my children will be surrounded by everyday heroes who will help them live in an enthusiastic and morally acceptable manner.

Ironically, I learn as much from my children as they do from me. My two young daughters have the same response every night when bedtime is announced. They look at my wife and me with total disbelief and respond, "Oh no, not again — do we have to?" They comply but not without an intense feeling of disappointment. Once my daughter got out of bed desperately trying to come up with an excuse to stay up a little later. She said, "Daddy, I can't get to sleep because my teeth are wet."

"Nice try, Kylee," I replied. "Now go to bed." I look forward to their nightly response to bedtime because it is a very good indication that they are trying to live each day to the fullest. Every minute that goes by is an opportunity for them to play, learn, and share the joy of life with someone else. What is my typical response when I go to bed? Perhaps they can remind me how to look forward to living life with a passion.

In turn, my gift to them is to do everything I can to ensure that in their world, character will count! And it has to start with me to do everything I can to be their everyday hero.

REFERENCES

Brooks, B.D. & Goble, F.G. (1997). *The Case for Character Education.* Northridge, CA: Studio 4 Productions.

Covey, Stephen R. (1994). *First Things First.* New York, NY: Simon & Schuster.

Covey, Stephen R. (1989). *The 7 Habits of Highly Effective People.* New York, NY: Simon & Schuster.

Josephson, M.S. (1997). *Making Ethical Decisions.* Marina del Rey, CA: Josephson Institute of Ethics.

Josephson, M.S. & Hanson, W. (1998). *The Power of Character.* San Francisco, CA: Jossey-Bass Inc.

Josephson, M.S. (2000). Character Development Seminars. Marina del Rey, CA: Josephson Institute of Ethics.

Lickona, T. (1991). *Educating for Character.* New York, NY: Bantam Books.

Lickona, T. (1983). *Raising Good Children.* New York, NY: Bantam Books.

Peck, M. Scott (1993). *Further Along the Road Less Traveled.* New York, NY: Simon & Schuster.

Ryan, K. & Bohlin, K.E. (1999). *Building Character in Schools.* San Francisco, CA: Jossey-Bass Publishers.